FUNNY MONEY

FUNNY MONEY

Bernard Hollowood

Foreword by Kenneth Fleet

MACDONALD AND JANE'S · LONDON

© Bernard Hollowood 1975

Published 1975 by Macdonald & Jane's
Macdonald & Co., (Publishers) Ltd.
Paulton House,
8 Shepherdess Walk, London N.1.

ISBN 0 356 08328 4

Printed and bound in Great Britain by The Pitman Press, Bath

CONTENTS

FOREWORD

According to my secretary I am not *particularly* nasty; I have a raincoat and I *may* sponge a little; certainly I pry. I don't think I lie but if I do it is not with dedication. If you have not guessed already, when you read this book you will gather I am a journalist. Perhaps I should apologise but in self-defence let me plead just two things. The subject of money is painfully serious but I believe it is also richly funny. Secondly, I had the wit to encourage Bernard Hollowood to prove it every Saturday in *The Daily Telegraph*.

All writers know how difficult it is to write humorous copy. A remark, let alone a thousand-word article or a book, that strikes one reader as funny may mortify another and baffle nine more. If you have not read Bernard Hollowood in *The Daily Telegraph* or seen his cartoons in *The Times*, this collection will convince you he has few rivals as a humorist. But like all the best humorous writers and cartoonists, he has a coherent set of personal values, a view of society as he believes it ought to be.

Funny Money is much more than just another funny book.

Kenneth Fleet

INTRODUCTION AND EXPLANATION

There was a time, believe it or not, when the BBC managed to get along without its *Money Programme* and when the business and financial sections of the newspapers, if they existed at all, were intended for the eyes of a tiny minority of investors and economic theoreticians. As I remember it, the deluge was heralded by the stock market boom of the 'sixties, the proliferation of unit trusts, the craze for mergers and take-over bids, the formation of private 'investment clubs' and a dramatic increase in financial advertising. Quite suddenly, the popular dailies launched new sections called 'Your Shares Today' or 'Investment Corner' and attempted to coach their baffled readers in such mysteries as yield, price-earnings ratio and 'times covered'; while their big brothers, the quality dailies and Sundays, offered whole new supplements devoted to business, economics and money in all its forms.

The boom stimulated advertising, particularly of hundreds of new unit trusts, income bonds and property bonds, and additional editorial prose was needed to decorate and separate the acres of ads. And a new literary form was developed to meet the need. There were informative articles on every aspect of the monetary scene – some lively and original, but the vast majority somewhat plodding and repetitive – and editors soon realised that the diet of porridge needed a flavouring of humour.

I like to think that I played a small pioneering hand in this business via the pages of *Punch* where, during and after the Hitler war, I was encouraged to write on such esoteric topics (for *Punch*) as 'An Economic Case-Book', 'British Industries at War' and 'Industrial Relations'. I had been trained as an economist and had worked both in industry and on *The Economist* newspaper, so I was writing from a certain amount of inside knowledge, and I enjoyed these literary endeavours more than any other form of writing. I was also a *Punch* cartoonist specialising in gags of a topical nature – especially those dealing in political and economic matters.

I returned refreshed to this dual existence as cartoonist and writer on economic affairs after I had completed eleven years as editor of *Punch* in 1968, and the two chief markets for my wares were now *The Times* (business section cartoons) and *The Daily Telegraph* (Money-Go-Round columnist). The material in this book is drawn almost exclusively from these sources, and I here and now acknowledge with thanks the help I have received from Hugh Stephenson, business editor of *The Times*, various editors of that paper's Business Diary and Kenneth Fleet, city editor of *The Daily Telegraph*.

I am particularly indebted to Kenneth Fleet for his kind foreword.

2

Economics, in my view, is concerned with uncommon commonsense. A person can become a competent economist merely by taking sufficient thought, though by such means he would be quite unable to pass economics exams set by those who consider the subject an abstruse science, an excuse for higher mathematics.

Difficulty arises when people convince themselves that economics is no more than *ordinary* commonsense, when they treat problems superficially and allow themselves to be hoodwinked by the strange commodity called money.

Money is a deceiver. We use it in our everyday language as a measure and a store of value; we believe in it so devoutly that we mistake it for real wealth and power. A man may hoard £50,000 and comfort himself with the notion that he can at least eat and drink without financial difficulty for the rest of his days. But his real savings are chimerical and are represented by nothing more substantial than a few figures in a bank account. The credit he has acquired with society may not be honoured. The citizens of the future may decide that his claim on their current output of goods – food and drink – is invalid. Every day such monetary claims are dishonoured by adulterating or cheapening the currency. By inflating. We now know all too well that £50,000 in the bank today is very unlikely to be worth £50,000 next year and may have dwindled to nothing by the year 2000 AD. Such changes occurred with extreme rapidity in Germany in the 'twenties.

We are led astray by language. We say that Christopher Wren built St Paul's, that Cosimo threw a bridge across the Arno, and, of course, we know that the structures in each case were erected by the labours of thousands of workers. But when we think of the cost of such projects we are quite ready to believe that the money was supplied out of existing stocks, that the cathedral and the bridge were built with money saved in the past, when in fact the *real* cost of the structures was the amount by which the general standard of living was *currently* reduced by the sidetracking of so much human skill and endeavour.

The Florentines who threw that bridge over the Arno could have been employed in many different ways. They could have been in the fields helping to improve crops, or they could have built hospitals or homes for the aged. The real cost of any human project lies in the 'deprived alternatives', the value of other uses to which the sweat and skill of all concerned *could* have been applied.

So when we praise great philanthropists we should remember that their generosity in establishing a college at

Oxbridge or building a hospital is quite meaningless. The labour that builds the hospital is transferred from other jobs and the general public pays for the new amenity by going without the produce or artefacts that might otherwise have been created.

In a true democracy there would be no room for the so-called benefactions of the rich. In a democracy the people, not one man, would decide upon the allocation of scarce resources, for as we have seen the cost of every project, whether it is the decision of one or many, lies on the shoulders of the whole community.

This argument might collapse if it were possible for the rich to accumulate savings in terms of hot dinners, clothing and material necessities. Then the employment of hundreds or thousands of men on some work of charity might be financed without reducing the general standard of living. But wealth does not consist of stores of hot dinners – only of financial claims on future production – and such claims can be converted into material wealth only by redirecting the labours of part of the day's working population.

Some years ago I startled all but a handful of students at a lecture given in North Carolina by stating that a millionaire would behave most responsibly by burning his pile. The campus chieftains were appalled by the idea because theirs was the conventional wisdom that equates paper wealth with *real* wealth. The students however had already written off the conventional wisdom as claptrap.

3

Before donning cap and bells let me continue in serious vein for a page or so. I am convinced that the friction in our society is due almost entirely to our system of income distribution. Pay differentials between rich and poor are far too wide. We are no longer two nations in matters of education and aspirations: we all watch the telly and are encouraged by commercials to live the good life of material prosperity. And the economic and industrial machine is so complex that it suffers breakdown when any of its human cogs fails to function satisfactorily.

I met a young economist not long ago. Personable, neat, neither short nor long back and sides. Told me he was fed up with people like Wilson and Keith Joseph, to mention only about 50 million, who are forever talking about the size of the national cake.

Why cake, for God's sake, when we've been told to tighten our belts and can expect no improvement in standard of living for two or more years. Cake and Marie Antoinette: image all wrong. We should be talking about the national loaf or crust.

However the young economist was prepared for argument's sake to stick with cake to represent national income, but insisted that its size is less important than its ingredients. National cake, he says, is not homogeneous. Largest slice consists of essentials for everyday existence, basic foods, clothes, heat, shelter, power. Call this Slice A. We all need a share of Slice A and we get one, though some get more than others.

Slice B is made up of semi-luxuries and inessentials, goods and services that most of us want and save up to buy. This slice includes TV sets, holidays on the Costa Brava, the odd bottle of plonk, extra clobber and an occasional paperback. Most people can share in Slice B if they've got strong unions, work overtime and save.

But there's a third slice, C, said my young LSE acquaintance, which consists solely of luxuries beyond the financial resources of all but (say) 10 per cent of the population. Ingredients: posh goods and services, sumptuous hotels and clubs (with servants galore), big cars, yachts, private swimming pools and tennis courts, expensive furniture, houses, flats, country cottages, furs, china, cutlery, napery and exotic foods and drinks obtainable at F & Mason. All expensive. You know the stuff, he said, champers, liqueurs, pate de foie gras, quails in aspic, caviar, everything you'd expect at a feast hosted by Lucullus.

Now we come to my point, he said. Slice C is produced by the mass of ordinary 4 and 5 type citizens, and not by those who consume it. It follows, surely, that all the workers engaged in producing Slice C are mugs, dupes of the system. They're providing goods and services that they can never hope to consume or use, so they're wasting their time and energy.

What they should be doing, my friend went on, is work to increase the size of Slices A and B. Not of the whole cake – just Slices A and B.

Let me say it again – because I don't think it's yet sunk into your conventional mind – the workers on Slice C are fools, crackpots, dolts. They know very well that slaves built the pyramids to the glory of individual kings, queens and princes; they know that workers in the Middle Ages were barely kept alive while they toiled on the construction of great cathedrals and great houses. They know that hungry men on a desert island would continue to fish and climb for coconuts rather than obey one man anxious to have a fine house or a yacht. And yet . . .

We've had it wrong all these years, talking about the *size* of the national cake: it's the *ingredients* of the cake that matter.

Well, that was quite a mouthful and I felt impelled after a time to make some token observation. So I told the young man that though I agreed with much of what he had to say Slice C of the national cake is important because it adds a rich dimension (oh, yes, I have enough maths to prove that dimensions can be rich) to the quality of life. People were kept afloat during the depression of the 'thirties by the dreamboat world of the cinema, and even today it does the poor and hungry good to see TV commercials in which girls' hair moves in luxurious slow motion, in which dumb animals are coaxed into consuming juicy chunks of meat, children stuff themselves with sweets, cakes and jellies, everybody has a car, a freezer, a washing-machine and a lover, and people ride aircraft as effortlessly as they once rode bikes.

I admitted that Slices A and B could be increased in size very considerably if all the people now employed on Slice C were transferred to work on them, but I pointed out that the existence of luxuries is necessary in order to make men envious, covetous and fiercely competitive.

Imagine a world, I said, where successful people cannot buy E-types, Mercs and Rolls-Royces, where they couldn't own two, three or more homes or have winter strawberries flown in from Florida or Tasmania. Dull, eh?

I tried to convince the young man that the size of the national cake was really less important than its quality.

But he wouldn't have it and called me a bourgeois, reactionary four-letter word.

4

Some serious ideas are embodied in the light pieces that follow, but in the main my intention has been to poke gentle fun at the economic and financial scene. Money is funny and its jargon can be endlessly fascinating.

I have adopted a non-political stance in these articles for the good reason that I have impermanent political convictions. I was bitterly disappointed by Labour's showing between 1964 and 1970 and I was horrified by Chancellor Barber's handling of taxation and currency in the last Conservative administration. Though both Labour and Conservatism tried unavailingly to introduce a statutory prices and incomes policy I am convinced that such a policy is necessary. The monopoly power of the unions is highly dangerous, for under modern conditions of capital-intensive production they can blackmail management into conceding wage claims that are injurious to the concept of fairer shares and almost certain to create inflation and unemployment.

We are not yet, however, ready for a statutory incomes policy, and regretfully I have to admit that the country will not see reason in this matter until it has suffered two or three shattering blows and setbacks.

1984 seems as likely a year as any for the introduction of economic sanity, fairer shares and for the abolition of a class system rooted in gross financial differentials.

5

If I poke fun at the City and its denizens and at big business it is because I see them as key figures and institutions in the human comedy.

In the public eye very few of us are employed honourably and are free from our share of the seven deadly sins. Nowadays we tend to disparage politicians as dealers in hot air and false promises. Economists are dismal jimmies unable to agree with each other and spouting platitudes disguised in jargon. Pedagogues? Well, at the level of the don they are remote, cloistered, cossetted and irrelevant and at the 'comprehensive' level they are idle white-collar workers with short hours, long hair and eternal holidays.

The bank managers and their staffs used to command considerable respect in any neighbourhood. A little of the mystery of money rubbed off on to them and they worked in dignified premises parading polished woods and marble. Now, however, the bank manager is the unpleasant satrap (ruled from head office) who gets tough about overdrafts and no longer fawns before customers with accounts in the black, while his clerks are – well, people who dole out cash as the fishmonger doles out fish. Estate agents next. No glory for them. Here are sharpies, middlemen, who intercede, intervene, between house-seller and house-buyer and charge the earth for unnecessary work, if tootling around in an E-type between house and house, property and property, can be dignified as work.

Come to think of it there are very few people we *do* respect these days. The clergy? No, silly lot of twits, people who should know what's what, but are too cowardly to come right out with it, to take sides, offend politicians and stone-age parishioners, if any. Policemen used to be Bobbies: now they are 'the fuzz'. Shopkeepers belong to that section of society derided by snobs as *trade* and the average customer regards them as profiteers who weigh their thumbs with the meat or groceries. We don't think too highly of accountants, and as for turf accountants or bookies they are almost on the fringe of the criminal classes. Scientists really are strange birds. They have no conscience and would cheerfully blow up the universe to prove the point in an essay consisting largely of footnotes.

Architects build boxes, battery premises for humans, and tear down the only bits of Britain that matter. Lawyers charge disgusting fees, run a closed shop and speak in a language incomprehensible to ordinary mortals. Most workers belong to unions which are for ever ready to hold the country to ransom, strike, picket, and obstuct the police whenever they feel their privileges challenged.

Soldiers? Either public school bullies or working-class riff-raff. The military (including the navy and air force) can't be trusted: they have funny ideas and might do a follow-my-leader behind some glib fascist scoundrel. Actors and actresses: no substance and no morals. Journalists: nasty, raincoated spongers, pryers, and dedicated liars.

So if the chaps who are something-in-the-City or in big business are mocked, they're in good company. And that includes . . .

Bernard Hollowood

PART 1
INVESTMENT
MOSTLY

RISING VALUE OF THE BILLET-DOUX

STAMPS, silver, Krugerrands, antiques, impressionists, Dutch masters, butterflies, dirty postcards . . . people looking for a hedge against inflation have tried them all. The other day a writer suggested a 'portfolio of canned foods' and this copy was promply reproduced by an American canning company as part of a convincing advertisement. But the latest source of financial security is said to be the *billet-doux* or love letter, and here, I think, I am in a position to offer desperate readers a certain amount of avuncular advice.

'He's on Mastermind *and terrified of being asked to define the Social Contract.'*

Obviously, the first line of action is to make a prolonged visit to the attic. That's where the family's old love letters usually end up. You may be lucky and discover that your grandfather had correspondence with Lily Langtry or your great-grandfather with Florence Nightingale. It's quite possible that your great-grandmother knew Lloyd George or Edward VII and there may be epistolary evidence to prove it. So you could be in the money.

Imagine it – the scene at Sotheby's as your little bundle of letters comes under the hammer! '£5,000 am I bid, six, seven, eight? Thank you, sir. May I say nine? Ten? Eleven? Done then at £11,000 . . .'

But suppose you've combed the attic and found nothing more exciting than your father's cricket cuttings and your wife's mother's knitting patterns copied from the *Lady's Companion*. What then? Are you excluded from the billet-doux business? Not necessarily.

My contacts with the famous have been sketchy. I once heckled Ramsay MacDonald in Hanley when he had just cut teachers' pay by 10 p.c., and in my teens I carried the suitcase of a lady member of the Russian ballet all the way from the Theatre Royal, Manchester, to her digs three miles away without saying a word. Then there was the time I got a crossed line and found myself talking briefly with the trainer of Rin Tin Tin and I still have a mark on my forehead where I was struck by a golf ball sliced by none other than Henry Cotton.

But my pride and glory is a postcard from Bernard Shaw. I have it framed in my study and I dare say it's now worth its weight in gold or carbon black. How did I acquire the postcard? Simple – I wrote to GBS with a question and the great man answered. If I'd had the sense years ago to write to other notabilities I might now be the proud possessor of postcards or letters from Ivor Novello, H.G. Wells, Jack Hobbs, Nazimova, Pola Negri, Stanley Baldwin, Constance Talmadge and Roscoe Arbuckle.

So you see it's up to you. With a bit of cunning you could now be laying down capital for your children and your children's children. All you need is a pen and a lot of effrontery.

Dear Miss Lollobrigida (you write), I have no right to confront you with this special request, but the fact is that you are my dreamboat princess. Ever since I first saw you on the silver screen I have known that you are and can be the only woman in my life. I adore you, and the fact that my love is hopeless and vain makes no difference to my feelings.

Don't worry: I am no nutcase and I shall never bother you again, but dare I hope that you will soothe my aching heart by penning me the briefest of missives? A note saying merely that I have your sympathy would give me something to live for. Yours in illicit devotion . . .

Identical letters to 150 of today's top women would almost certainly net you at least 30 replies, and these by the year 2000 AD could be worth a bomb.

Writing to distinguished men calls for subtlety of a different order.

Dear Mr Wedgwood Benn (Mr Thorpe or Mr Whitelaw), I am not in the habit of writing to celebrities, but I am nearing the end of my days and before I pass into the Great Beyond I should like you to know that only my admiration for your work and my interest in your career have made my declining years worth living. In my humble opinion you are the greatest living Englishman, or should I say Briton. I write in the shaky hand of a woman who has already heard the Call, and if you could find it in your heart to scribble a line or two by return your generosity would undoubtedly add another week or so to my useless existence. Yours most faithfully . . .
P.S. I don't enclose stamped, addressed envelope because I want to see my name written by you and I want to know that the stamp adheres with the aid of your very own spittle.

It is not unknown for people to discover love letters at jumble sales. You buy a decrepit trilby, once the property of Lord Nexus, and tucked inside the inner band you find a letter beginning 'My own sweet embraceable You . . .' and ending 'Yours till hell freezes over, "Boo-boo." ' The writer of the letter could conceivably be the late Lady Nexus or it could be any one of the ladies mentioned in Peer's Progress, Lord Nexus's ghosted autobiography. If Lord N is still alive you deposit the letter in your safe and leave it in your will to a grandchild. If Lord N is dead you nip round to Christie's or Sotheby's and consult their manuscripts expert.

Personally, I make an inventory of my *billets-doux* every year or so, keep them up to date as one would a portfolio of investments. I make sure that the purple patches haven't faded, get rid of moths and ink in lines of endearment suffering from mildew.

SPECULATORS ANONYMOUS

ALMA CARBON looked at the heap of stones she had collected and wondered whether it was big enough. She was weary, almost asleep on her feet, but she had to be sure. Twice before she had been certain of success, and twice her plans had been ruined at the last moment by the automatic skills vested in the muscles of her arms and legs.

Very slowly and deliberately she began to pocket the pieces of flint and ragstone – the fruits of her long and arduous search. The paucity of rocks in the park had surprised her. It was now almost dark and to locate the last of her cache she had to put on her reading glasses.

And now she was ready. She turned towards the water and shuffled forward . . .

'I'd been watching you for most of the afternoon,' said P.K. Tellwright, proffering another cigarette. 'Couldn't make you out for a long time. Even thought you were dotty. And now you tell me you've never heard of SA. Well, well! We must improve our public relations. Are you feeling strong enough to push on, or would you like another cup of tea?'

'Oh, no thank you,' said Mrs Carbon. 'I really don't know how to thank you. But I'm quite sure I shall be all right now, after your wonderful advice. I mustn't take up any more of your time. Goodnight, and thank you again.'

'Advice?' said P.K. Tellwright. 'My dear lady, you mustn't say that. I'm not qualified to give advice. I'm only a member, not a counsellor. And you are not saying goodnight to me until I've seen you safely in the hands of Mr Trott. When you're ready . . .'

'I want you to stop feeling sorry for yourself, Mrs Carbon – or may I call you Alma?' said Paul Trott, consulting his notes. 'Practically everyone who comes to us for help has felt suicidal at some time or other. Your case is typical, and I'm almost certain we can help you – if you let us.'

'Why, of course,' said Alma. 'I'll do anything you say. I'm so ashamed of myself, causing so much trouble.'

'Wrong again, I'm afraid,' said Paul. 'We *like* trouble. You've got to remember that everyone here has suffered just as you are suffering. Every member of Speculators Anonymous has felt as hopeless about the future as you do now. Mr Tellwright tells me this was, or would have been, your third attempt at suicide. Would you care to talk about it? Say yes or no, I shan't mind.'

'Whether I was serious or not about suicide,' said Alma, 'I don't know. You see, as a girl I got into the regional finals of the 100 yards trudgen championship and might even have made the England team if I'd stuck to it. So although I put weights in all my pockets I managed to swim around long enough to be picked up. Of course, this evening might have been different. It was dark.'

'Would you like another coffee, Alma?' said Paul. 'Sure? Well, let me tell you a bit more about SA. Few people understand that speculation can be a disease, a chronic disease. Something like one in ten of investors is either a speculator or a potential speculator, and the line between the two is not easy to draw. It's insidious. Thirty years ago it wasn't even recognised . . . But I can see you want to say something. Do go on, please. Unburden yourself.'

'My father introduced me to investing when I was very young – started me off with a little portfolio of my own before I left school,' said Alma. 'And I was perfectly normal until I went to Cambridge. There I used to spend every minute studying the market, buying and selling. I bought rubbish, shares in "shell" companies that looked dead; I bought shares on the strength of astrological predictions and in anticipation of expected rumours of takeover bids. I was completely hooked.'

'And you lost everything?'

'In the end, yes. But enough of my wildest speculations came good to satisfy my craving. I could drop £5,000 and make £200 and feel really high. At 22 I went bankrupt and walked into the Serpentine with my jumper full of roofing tiles.'

'Poor dear.'

'Then I married a wealthy estate agent and lived normally for nearly two years. In 1963, like a fool, I invested £30 of my housekeeping money in a unit trust and . . .'

'A chronic situation,' said Paul. 'Once you'd sampled the thrill again you couldn't stop. You started speculating like crazy and lost everything once more.'

'Including my husband,' sobbed Alma.

'All right, that's enough for now,' said Paul. 'Let's go into the common room – sin bin, we call it – and meet some of your fellow sufferers.'

They made their way upstairs to a large smoke-filled room. It contained seven tables and at each sat four patients playing Monopoly for used matchsticks. The atmosphere was electric. There was no noise, but every eye burned with a fierce acquisitive flame. The patients were of all ages and both sexes. There were mountains of match boxes stacked all round the walls.

'It may seem odd,' said Paul, 'but it works. Here members of SA give vent to their addiction, play out their phantasies. It's therapeutic. As a safety measure I insist on every match being struck before use.'

'But one can lose even at Monopoly,' said Alma.

'Oh, yes, we cater for that too,' said Paul. 'If you watch for a few minutes you'll see for yourself.'

Seconds later there was an unearthly groan from an elderly bald-headed man at table 5. He staggered to his feet and to the window, opened it and threw himself into the night with a piercing scream.

'Not to worry,' said Paul. 'The yard is eight feet deep in sponge rubber. The ritual "suicide" seems to satisfy some deep longing in SAs. He'll be back in a minute ready for another game. He'll borrow enough to buy a few dozen boxes and start again.'

'How marvellous,' said Alma. 'I'd like to try it. May I? Will you join me?'

'I'm afraid not,' said Paul. 'I'm the only one who's not allowed to play. It would be unethical. You see, I happen to be not only the founder of SA but the sales manager of the Britannica-Trott Match Company.'

WHO CRASHED FROM THE SKYSCRAPERS?

WE ALL know what women do when depressed. They rush off to the shops and buy themselves a new hat or handbag, or they indulge in an expensive hair-do or facial. A lady of my acquaintance suffered such frequent bouts of depression during a prolonged period of amorous indecision that she acquired no fewer than 237 handbags: She is now the proprietor of Lily's of Regent Street and American visitors claim that the shop is unequalled for the range and quality of its bags and other accessories. She remains a spinster.

Men suffering from the blues are supposed to resort to drink. Well, yes, some do. But I've discovered recently that many City establishments other than pubs thrive on misery. Mr Johnston of Henry's, Cyril of the Vauxhall Sauna, Elle and Sie of Man o'Hair, Eastcheap, and Tony of Groomrite will all tell you that a dip of five points in the industrial index means a sharp increase in takings and a lot of overtime for their employees.

Henry's is of course the City tailor, reputedly the originator of the old stockbroking uniform of black jacket and striped pants. 'It's all blue pin-stripes today,' says Mr Johnston. 'Haven't sold a uniform for years, though the cartoonists continue to draw tycoons garbed as of old. It was Lord Gargle who started it, you know. Very forgetful, his lordship. Like Harold Macmillan who launched the vogue for the black bow-tie *under* the shirt collar. Mr M., you'll recall, turned up at a party at the Connaught in '57 looking a perfect wreck – buttons undone and tie hidden by his shirt points; and Selwyn Lloyd, quick as a flash, tucked *his* tie behind *his* collar, to make the leader's carelessness seem like a very "with it" eccentricity. And so, one after the other, all the males present followed suit and a new fashion was born.

'Well, Lord Gargle, who was *very* absent-minded, went to the City one day properly dressed in correct funeral black except that he'd still got his striped pyjamas on! He must have looked a right Charlie, but nobody mentioned his gaffe and the rest of the Bentinck & Gargle board changed diplomatically into stripes as soon as possible. And from that day until VJ Day the City uniform was black jacket and striped pants.

'Our business is *very* sensitive. By 12.15 any morning I can tell you to within half a point what the FT index is doing. If it's down, the swatches of heather mixtures and tweeds are being thumbed like nobody's business and the tie department is flogging silk paisleys by the gross.'

The Vauxhall Sauna is next door to Henry's and on bearish days traffic between the two establishments is brisk. A jobber will try on a sports coat a couple of sizes too small for his girth and pop next door to lose an inch or so of adipose tissue in the Vauxhall caldarium. Then pop back to Henry's for another fitting, and so on.

Cyril, manager of the Vauxhall Sauna, has a tape machine in his office and adjusts temperatures according to the movement of gilts. 'Have to!' he explained to me. 'When there's a rush on customers with faces as long as fiddles want instant action! If I kept them waiting they'd commit suicide. So I increase the throughput of bodies by upping the therms. They're in and out like piston rods. Matter of fact, on really bad days (for the market) we get so overheated that customers strip off even in the waiting rooms and bars. In July, when the index dropped like a stone three days running, Henry's, next door, was complaining that the heat from our place was melting the plastic of their suit-covers, and we had the fire brigade hosing the walls and roof all afternoon.'

The chief attractions at Man o' Hair are two dazzlers – one Gallic, one Teutonic – known as Elle and Sie. They're not merely decorative; they're expert psychotherapists and know exactly how to lift clients out of the doldrums. They change their dress hour by hour according to the marked bargains count. When business on the floor is bad they increase their decolletage and shorten their minis, and there were days in August this year when the two plimsoll lines, so to speak, were barely an inch or two apart.

'Mind you,' said Alfredo, owner of Man o'Hair, 'Elle and Sie never manicure. Physical contact with customers would be disastrous. So we employ somewhat plainer girls – Cuticle Cuties, we call 'em – on that side of the business. It's been a very hot summer, as you know, and there's been a terrific slump in the sale of toupees and hair-pieces. In fact baldness has become fashionable again, especially since we introduced our special scalp-hair remover at ten guineas a jar. Marvellous thing, psychology. Our most popular cut or style at present is the Half Tonsure – that is, a naked dome with a few residual hairs at back and sides. A bald insurance broker gets tucked into his chair and asks for a "Half T," the hairdresser makes snipping noises with his scissors and a few complimentary remarks, and the broker coughs up £2.50 and feels a genuine glow of good grooming.'

'You must be joking! Look up the trains and flights ourselves? Book our own hotel in Majorca? All by ourselves?'

All of which merely demonstrates that every cloud etcetera. But is the converse true? I mean, do the above-mentioned establishments suffer when the stock market is thriving and bargains are being driven thick and fast?

Yes, no doubt about it. Let me quote Mr Johnston again.

'When they're feeling euphoric,' he says. 'City gents couldn't care less about appearances and grooming. They never leave their phones and computers. Don't bother even about lunch. Send out for sandwiches of brown bread and smoked salmon and use the office booze cabinet. Hair, nails and waist-lines are neglected and they certainly can't spare the time to see one of my visiting tailors. During the boom of 1972, when the index was around the 530 mark, Waterloo Station looked like a doss-house between nine and 10 in the morning as trains from the Surrey stockbroker belt disgorged hordes of grinning tatterdemalion commuters.

'You've never seen such specimens. Dusty bowlers, hair over their collars, cuffs deckled with ball-point jottings, season tickets stapled to breast pockets for speedy platform egress, ragged moustaches, untouched crossword puzzles, odd socks, down-at-heel shoes and slept-in suits. The lot!'

'Show me a man's hands,' says Alfredo, 'and I can tell you what's cooking – base rates, indices, trade figures, order books, industrial stoppages, the entire economic and financial scene. Nails rounded and polished to perfection mean gloom. Nails neglected and in mourning mean boom.'

So all those stories about financiers crashing to their death from Wall Street skyscrapers in the Great Depression of 1929 are fairy tales. The hurtling bodies (historians please note) were those of bartenders, hairdressers, tailors, chiropodists, manicurists, masseurs and psychiatrists who had finally cracked under the strain of being monstrously overworked.

HAVE A CARE FOR YOUR SHARE

NATHANIEL SCOWLE was an almost exemplary husband. He was a good provider, mowed the lawn on Saturday mornings, praised his wife's cooking at every meal, did the drying-up whenever the dishwasher went on the blink, remembered his children's and grandchildren's birthdays, made early morning tea on Sundays and bank holidays, drank in moderation, let his wife decide which telly programmes they watched, always left the bath as clean as he found it, and handled all household accounts without a murmur.

Esther Scowle appreciated her husband's sterling qualities and found him wanting in only one respect. All her friends and neighbours journeyed abroad for three or four weeks in the summer, to the Continent or to resorts as far afield as Cyprus, Florida and Honolulu, and these breaks in the suburban routine of Dorking provided them with small talks of an anticipatory, reflective, scatological or anecdotal nature for the greater part of the year. Esther always wanted to holiday overseas, but Nathaniel would not budge from 'Highlea,' Croxton Avenue.

He was not mean. On the contrary, he urged her to travel, pleaded with her to pack a bag and taxi to Heathrow whenever he detected tears.

'But I can't go alone,' she would say. 'Whatever would people think? Besides, you need a holiday abroad as much as I do. Other men manage to get away – why can't you?'

'Don't let's go into all that again,' said Nathaniel. 'Our investments need watching and I can't do that properly if I'm stuck in some God-forsaken place where they don't take English newspapers and where I can't get on the blower to my brokers in a hurry.'

'That's a ridiculous excuse and you know it! How often do you contact your broker? How often have you bought or sold a share in the past month? Not once!'

'That's not the point, Esther. Things happen like lightning in the investment business, and if you're not on the spot you can lose everything. Just like that!' And he snapped his fingers at her.

'Well, if you're so scared, why not sell all your shares and put the proceeds into building societies or something for a month? Then after our holiday you could get the money out and buy your shares back again.'

'Wouldn't help,' he said. 'Dealing in shares is expensive. But what a fool I should look if the shares rocketed while we were away and I couldn't get them back. No. I've thought of everything – investment trusts, unit trusts, bonds, leaving everything in Chapman's hands – and it's no good. I'm sorry, Ess, but there it is.'

And there it was, the same old row week in, week out until one day, in May, 1970, Esther packed her bags and set off for Malta. She left her husband a note stating that unless he joined her at the Rialto Hotel, Valleta, within three days she would never return. Ultimatum.

'What's the use of raising false hopes? You know as well as I do that tax collectors never go on strike.'

Nathaniel spent a whole day brooding and the best part of the following day working out the cost of daily return flights between Heathrow and Malta. He found that he could cover the 1,300 miles in six hours so that the 12.30 p.m. plane would see him in Valleta by 6.30 in good time for dinner with his wife. Then there was a night flight leaving Malta at midnight and getting him home in time for possible business transactions by 6 a.m. The schedule was expensive, very, but it would keep his marriage alive.

Esther was overjoyed when he turned up on the third day,

even when he apprised her of his plans to commute. A man who would travel through half of every day and night to be with his wife was undoubtedly a devoted husband.

Only one of Scowle's shares wobbled by more than 2p during the strange holiday – Quindustries International, a conglomerate operating in all five continents – and even with this investment the change was nothing like significant enough to tempt Nathaniel to trade. But the month completely upset the rhythm of life at 'Highlea' and shook its owners out of their dull routine.

Newspaper reporters stationed at Heathrow soon become inquisitive about blue-jowled men who arrive daily at 6 a.m., and by the end of the second week Nathaniel was under scrutiny. Questioned, he was loath to admit the real reason for his journeying, appeared flustered and querulous and mumbled something about a business deal. A sharp young man from the *Chronicle* turned in a speculative piece about tax avoidance (called 'The Sky is Their Tax Haven') in which he suggested that tycoons spending half their lives in the air can't be domiciled terrestrially anywhere long enough to come within the jurisdiction of national taxmen.

So pictures of the 'mystery financier,' a furtive, hunted, middle-aged man with a bulging brief-case and weary eyes, appeared in the gossip columns.

When these photographs and stories reached Malta the gigolos casing the Rialto promptly made tracks for Mrs Tycoon, and one of them, Giuseppe Valdini, managed to kindle romantic thoughts in Esther by his flattery and attentiveness. Esther, once a prefect at Benenden, was incurably honest and at the first opportunity confessed her infatuation to her winging husband.

Nathaniel, already bemused by his burgeoning notoriety, accepted the news with dazed indifference and on his next flight to London made a play for an impressionable air hostess thirty years his junior. It was the first time Sandra had been pinched other than flirtatiously by a tycoon featured in the papers and she was impressed both physically and financially.

By mutual consent the month of commuting was extended, though Nathaniel now spent his hours in Valleta at a motel called 'the Roaring Forte,' and a few weeks later the Scowles agreed on an amicable separation, sold 'Highlea,' flogged all the investments and shared the proceeds.

Strangely enough, the new pairings worked. Esther financed Giuseppe in a plumbing and decorating business he had long coveted, and Sandra persuaded Nathaniel to study economics with the Open University.

Three months after the disposal of Nathaniel's portfolio the FT index dived nearly a hundred points, from 463 to 377 in next to no time.

Nat never went abroad again and Sandra was content to stay put. She had logged enough miles and reached her destination, and she saw no point in Nat pushing his luck a second time in foreign parts.

BE LOYAL TO SHARES-IT COULD JUST PAY

DOES the name Maintrace mean anything to you? Ambrose Maintrace? No, well I didn't think it would, but you never know. His name used to appear in the newspapers pretty frequently a few years ago, and I think he was seen occasionally on the box. I suppose I remember him because I still admire his system, and I know that if I had his drive and determination I would adopt it.

Most of us like to support the companies in which we invest by buying their products or services. Thus I keep tabs on Distillers by dutifully sinking a daily ration of gin and something. It is important, I feel, to make sure that the quality is maintained from month to month, day to day and hour to hour.

Maintrace differed from the ordinary investor in that he refused to buy *anything* unless he owned shares in the company producing it. He was inflexible in his resolve, even though his system often caused him embarrassment and sometimes made him suffer genuine privation.

I knew him slightly, for we were members of the same Bunny Club and would trade chat at the bar. He favoured the bar because it was dimly lit and allowed his somewhat unprepossessing appearance to pass almost unnoticed. One evening I was surprised to observe that his navy double-breasted was horribly worn, shredded at the cuffs and holed at the elbows. I asked whether he had been gardening.

'I'm in a bit of a fix,' he said. 'I've always bought my clothes at the 5,000 Pence Tailors because I've invested in them for years. Unfortunately, they've now been taken over by Gennel's and I don't approve. I've told my broker to sell my shares at 53p or better, but the damn things have been no higher than 47p for more than a year, and I can't very well patronise Gennel's whose suits are execrable. So my wardrobe is threadbare and until I can invest in a decent tailoring share I have to go about looking like a tramp.'

For a time I saw nothing of Maintrace. Then I bumped into him in the Long Room at Lord's and bought him lunch in the Tavern. Well, that's not quite accurate. He sat with me in the Tavern restaurant while I took lunch and, to the disgust of the waitress, he munched the egg sandwiches he'd brought with him.

'These people get their grub from —' he said (and he mentioned two names famous in catering). 'And of course I only eat the produce of Frescofare. I've had a slice of their equity for years.'

'But what happens,' I said, 'when you're hungry and there's

no Frescofare supermarket within reach?'

'I go without,' he said. 'Bit awkward, but I manage. I had a few days in Scotland last month, golfing, and lived entirely on Glen McCool products. Frescofare hasn't crossed the border yet.'

If this was a gentle hint, I took it. I finished the bottle of claret myself while Maintrace washed down his egg sandwiches with a succession of Glen McCools and splash.

'You must think I'm a queer fish,' he said, 'but I see no sense in supporting the shares of competing companies by buying their stuff. It goes against the grain.' By which I suppose he meant barley.

At stumps he asked me whether he could give me a lift and we sauntered to the Nursery car park where a sumptious Silver Cloud awaited us. I made appropriate noises of appreciation and covetousness.

'Mad, really,' he said. 'Who ever heard of an advertising copywriter owning a Rolls! But Rolls-Royce happens to be the only motor manufacturer whose shares appeal to me, so it had to be a Rolls or nothing. It won't be mine until 1980.'

I asked him what make of car he'd driven before the Rolls-Royce which was patently new.

'Didn't have one,' he said. 'My father left me a few shares in Raleigh so we had a tandem bike. Mind you, my wife hated it, and when the children came along it wasn't much use.'

This was the first mention of a Mrs Maintrace and I was puzzled.

'Hey,' I said, 'this funny investment system of yours – does your wife have to fit in with it?'

'Of course, be stupid otherwise, wouldn't it? Anyway, that's how I got *her*, if you see what I mean. I bought a few speculative shares in Cheviot Airways ten years back and made a couple of trips from Gatwick to Renfrew to check up on the company's efficiency. And Debby was one of their air hostesses.'

'So you're stuck with her until you get rid of the Cheviot shares?' I said with an explanatory grin.

'That's what *she* says,' said Maintrace. 'She's a good wife, wouldn't dream of buying anything from a competitor. We have a little meeting once a month, the two of us, when I give her the latest on my portfolio. But don't let that fancy word portfolio deceive you. I'm a relatively poor man for an investor. I own about a quarter of my house, one twelfth of the Rolls, and the cash value of the portfolio at this moment is only £3,087.50. And that includes 25 different shares!'

It was shortly after our Lord's encounter that Maintrace hit the headlines . . . 'Copywriter in Copyright Rumpus.'

An interesting story. Maintrace had produced a marvellous advertisement for Klober's Jam – a brilliant jingle that looked well in print and sounded catchy as a TV commercial. But just as Maintrace was giving birth to this masterpiece his employers lost the Klober account and offered their services – and Maintrace's jingle – to another jam manufacturer, Hedges and Croft of Worcester. The offer was accepted and Maintrace was horrified. You see, he had a few shares in Klober's but none in Hedges and Croft, and he refused to allow the jingle to be used for the new client.

The agency argued that it held full copyright in all the work of their employees, while Maintrace produced a document to the effect that his work was to be restricted to certain named accounts.

The ensuing litigation was settled eventually – out of court. The agency put Maintrace on the board and made him head of the Creative Department, and Hedges and Croft presented him with 1,000 50p ordinary shares standing at 137p.

When I last saw Maintrace – at Lord's – he was driving a Mini.

'You've sold the Rolls then?' I said.

'No, the wife uses it,' he said. 'I find this thing much more convenient.'

'So you bought shares in Leyland?'

'Not exactly,' he said. 'My system was getting a bit tricky, so I bought a raft of unit trusts with investments in just about everything. I check up on them occasionally just to make sure and it seems I'm now a shareholder in more or less everything.'

'But you still recommend the system?' I said.

'Naturally,' he said. 'Look what it did for me. I'm chairman of Europa Advertising, President of the Advertising Guild, own a town house, two farms, a Picasso and a Kandinsky and can get to Lord's any time I want to. Oh, yes, I still believe in buying the share behind the product and the product behind the share.'

BLUEPRINT FOR A NEW INVESTMENT SYSTEM

LIKE every small investor – active small investor, I mean – I spend a certain amount of time each day scanning the prices. It is a harmless pastime. Currently there are about two dozen companies in which I have a personal stake (don't be fooled by the grandiloquence of that word stake) and during the couple of minutes it takes me to locate them I experience two dozen momentary changes of mood. As a rule these are infinitesimally small and could not, I think, be detected by the most sensitive of measuring devices.

The shocks to my system are tiny because my portfolio is arranged in such a way that plus signs are almost automatically cancelled by minus signs. You see, all my bets are **hedged**.

When my stake in McDrip Rainwear depreciates in value I know for a certainty that CG Suntan Products will appreciate commensurately. If my tea shares lose a penny or two I can be sure that my coffee shares will make good the deficit. And so on. It's an unexciting portfolio, dull in fact, but that's the way it has to be.

So you will be puzzled if I tell you that I *exult* and fall about with happiness when certain shares nosedive. It's not a thing I'm proud of, but confession is supposed to be good for the soul and I've wanted to get this thing off my chest for a long time.

On Wednesday I had *two* boiled eggs for breakfast and followed them with a celebratory cigar. Why? Because Pinto Mines had dipped 15p. I have no Pinto shares. Four years ago, when they stood at 320p, I was strongly advised to buy them by an Australian cricketer.

We were at this party and the fellow had been dancing with my wife for almost an hour. At my time of life jealousy is ridiculous so as I waited at the bar and watched through narrowed eyes I turned my thoughts to pleasant matters like tax rebates, bonus issues and the economic concept of consumer surplus.

'Hope you didn't mind, cobber?' he said, when at long last they retired from the floor. 'I needed the exercise. See you at the Oval on Saturday.'

My wife was livid.

'Why couldn't you have been civil?' she snarled. 'The man was just getting interesting. He has real inside information about mining shares.'

I laughed. 'I suppose he tipped Poseidon, eh?' I said.

'No, but he urged me to buy something called Pinto Mines. His father's their banker. They're all set for lift-off. We'd be fools if we didn't nibble.'

Well, I didn't nibble and for four years I've watched Pinto soar out of my reach. They climbed to £27.50 and never once slipped or stalled. Sheer agony. My wife, thank heavens, doesn't follow the prices – so I was spared the lash of her tongue, but until last Wednesday I slept in a bed of nettles, tortured by the pricking of a frustrated acquisitive instinct.

So Wednesday was a red letter day. If Pinto shares fall *every* day by 15p they'll be down to 320p (the price I could have bought them at) in less than six months. I can't wait.

I am as patriotic as the next man, but my sadness at the continuing decline of British Leatherware shares is more than offset by my smug satisfaction in the knowledge that I have resisted the temptation to buy them whenever they have been heavily tipped over the past few years. In 1969 I had almost decided to invest £200 in BL. The signs were propitious. My method (at the time) decreed that I should seek refuge for my £200 with the first company whose initials matched those of seven (magic number!) postal correspondents. By August 12, British Leatherware, represented by Betty Livingstone, Bruce Lovatt, Brian Levine, Bill Lowndes, Barbara Limpett and Bunty Latimer had notched six names and was way out in front of all other contenders. RTZ, another candidate company on my list, had not been supported by a single correspondent, and ICI with, Izaac Charles Ibbotson, had only one vote.

'We see the wage claim as a tug-of-war between your liquidity and ours.'

It seemed all over. Then out of the blue I suddenly received eight letters signed by Magnus Graham, one of Her Majesty's commissioners of inland revenue. Eight! Three were final demand notices relating to 1966, two for 1967 and three more for 1968. Magnus Graham! MG. In no time at all I decided that this was a favourable portent and my money went off without delay to the M & G General unit trust. British Leatherware had been pipped by a short head.

And I have not regretted my decision. My watch strap is a BL product, but I am not as upset as I should be when I observe that BL shares continue their ungainly slide.

My 'correspondence' method of selecting shares for investment may not seem particularly scientific. Nevertheless it works. Last year after a close struggle Marks and Spencer just got home in front of Midland Bank, British Oxygen and Johnson Richards and left my other nominee Zambia Copper voteless.

For those of you who prefer a more serious system I would recommend the investment plan that I used in the early sixties. This is essentially a plan for the summer months, for it depends on a careful study of the scores in county cricket matches. The investor writes down the names of the first seven batsmen to score hundreds during the season, assembles the initial letters of their surnames and tries to arrange them, anagram fashion, to spell the name of a listed share. One year, thanks to Boycott, Edrich, Edwards, Cowdrey, Harvey, Armstrong and May, I fashioned the word Beecham and as a result acquired a very useful and profitable toehold in the pharmaceutical business.

Even more academic is my version of the 'chartist' system in which I convert the month's first prize-winning Premium Bond number into letters of the alphabet (A=1, B=2, and so on) and invest heavily if they happen to spell out the name of a listed share. In 1967 (I think it was) the digits of the May winner were 20519315 which I divided thus 20, 5, 19, 3, 15 and translated into Tesco. I was so pleased with this psychic tip that I sold my car and invested the resultant £420 in the food chain – and I have profited considerably by the deal.

Admittedly my methods are not for everybody. Brokers ridicule them. City editors are apt to scoff. Yet they do seem to bring results. (Send £500 and s.a.e. for my pamphlet Investment Can be Fun.)

WHEN BAD NEWS DOESN'T MEAN SELL

AS A MAN with a few shares in this and that – and I *mean* a few – I take a very poor view of the recent behaviour of some of my investing colleagues. Talk about over-reacting! They hear that Joe Gormley of the NUM has bought a home candlemaking outfit and they instruct their brokers to sell like mad and knock another 10 points off the FT index. Then there's a rumour that a senior representative of Saudi Arabia has been seen smiling at Ted Heath and the investors scramble to *buy*, like alcoholics a minute before closing time.

It's *indecent*! In normal times – that is, about one week in every dozen – I rather fancy myself as a City prophet. At the end of the 1 o'clock news summary on Radio 3 the reader trots out the latest on the index and more often than not (in normal times, remember) I can forecast which way the City sheep have turned with an accuracy that undermines my scepticism of telepathy. 'On the Stock Exchange,' he says, 'business was dull and the FT index was down by 3 points.' Just as I'd predicted from a careful reading of the morning papers! Exactly!

Subconsciously, I'd listed such bull points as the fine weather, Brian Clough having a sore throat, Frank Sinatra thinking of making a come-back, there being no further news about a reputed oil-slick off Weymouth, National Savings being up a trifle on last month, Miss Universe being on the evening's telly, labour troubles in Japan's car industry, the end of a three weeks' strike of veterinary surgeons in Lossiemouth, and a rumour that North Sea oil will have a slightly higher octane value than originally forecast; and I'd set against them such bear points as soccer attendances being down 23,000 on last year, a hint that The Mousetrap might move to a smaller theatre, the continuation of an unofficial strike of midwives in

Anglesey, and a leading article advocating stiffer death duties. And I'd struck a balance of exactly 3 points in favour of the bears!

Amazing really! If you don't believe me, ask my wife. She'll tell you how annoying I can be when I chip into the news a fraction ahead of the announcer with my 'and the FT index was down 3 points.'

'Think you're clever, don't you?' she usually says.

'Not particularly,' I say, 'I take no credit for the supreme efficiency of my subconscious.'

But there are days, weeks even, when my powers are definitely in abeyance, and then my wife really enjoys my discomfiture. The other day, for example, there seemed to be very little in the papers, and when the 1 o'clock news came round I made my usual confident prediction.

'Pass the mustard, darling,' I said. 'Ah, here we are – the index at noon was half a point down. Betcha!'

'. . . another bad day on the Stock Exchange,' said the news reader, 'with the index falling by no fewer than 17 points.'

'Ho-ho!' said my wife. 'So Mr Cleversticks can come a cropper! Still, you're not too bad – only 16½ points out.'

'Will you pass the mustard, *please*?' I hissed.

Now why do investors – oh, yes, *and* jobbers – over-react? Because they're utterly insensitive, that's why. Most of us are kept in check by fear of embarrassment. We think twice before phoning the broker or the bank manager because we're sentient beings who care what others think about them. Take me, for example. For a long time now I've had grave doubts about Conway Cement and, as everyone knows, it's been slipping recently by as much as 3p every day. I could have sold them three months ago at 147p and I could buy them again today for as little as 35p. But I've done nothing about them because I *know*, or think I do, that I should find the bank manager's reactions to a deal thoroughly humiliating . . .

'Hello! Could I have a word with Mr Tomlinson. Oh, that *is* Mr Tomlinson! Good morning, I was thinking of getting rid of my Conway Cement holding.'

'Yes, sir?' (*Thinks: 'His Conway Cement holding! I doubt whether he's got more than 50 shares. He's running scared. Probably read that bit in last week's Economist about them.'*)

'They're in pretty poor shape, so I think it might be wise to unload a few of them.'

'Yes, sir?' (*Thinks: 'Unload! My gawd, this is rich! A few of them? I'll bet he's going to pretend he doesn't know how many shares he's got.'*)

'So I wondered if you'd mind telling me what my holding is. You have the share certificates, of course. For safe keeping. Don't bother now if you're busy: any time will do.'

'No trouble at all, sir. Just a moment.' (*Thinks: 'Just as I thought, the little perisher . . . Ah, yes, 60 lousy shares!'*) 'You there, Mr Hollowood? I've got a list of your investments in front of me and you appear to have 60 Conway Cement 25p A shares.'

'Oh, as few as that? I suppose I must have flogged some of them and forgotten. Well, I don't want to disturb the market unduly, so I won't unload the lot. Will you sell half of them for me – at, say, 35 or better?'

'Sell 30 Conway Cement A shares at 35. Right you are sir, I'll get on to our broker and phone you back.' (*Thinks: 'He doesn't want to start a bear slide! Really why the hell doesn't he put his money in the Post Office and let me get on with some real work!'*)

Of course, I'm not saying that my bank manager *would* think like that, but that's how I imagine him reacting. And I couldn't face the prospect.

That's why I've sold no shares for years and why I'm unlikely to sell any in the future. And there are thousands of investors just like me. The FT index wobbles about between 500 and 300 and I watch the damn thing as if my life depended on it. It's mad, crazy, idiotic!

Still, I suppose it's a good thing that some investors under-react when so many of them behave like fairground hucksters. The insensitive louts!

ARE YOU ASHAMED OF YOUR SHARES?

SOME investors – but not too many – are wondering what to do with the shares of companies whose social policy they deplore. A company's products may be considered nasty, its attitude to its workers may seem barbarous or the countries with whom it trades may practise unmentionable practices: there may be a dozen reasons for a shareholder to feel uneasy about or ashamed of his investment.

One such shareholder lists possible lines of action. The shares could be sold and the proceeds pocketed. But this money would, he feels, be 'tainted.' The shares could be surrendered, handed back to the company, or they could be given away either to some charity or to an organisation known to be campaigning against the social evil of which the company is guilty.

He then, very sensibly, asks for my advice.

Well, the problem is one with which I am painfully familiar. Hardly a week, it seems, goes by without some company getting into my black books. The fools in charge declare a reduced dividend or allow its shares to lose value, and immediately my dander is up. My first reaction is to wash my hands of the business by selling out, but on second thoughts I usually decide to give the idiots a second, third or fourth chance.

This decision is arrived at when I have reminded myself that the company, its manager, chairman and board of directors don't give a damn whether I own the shares or not. Why should they? They don't know me from Adam, never see me and, since the shares are 'fully paid,' can expect nothing from me. Even Cary Le Mayer, as you will see, doesn't give a damn.

I learned my lesson some years ago when a company infuriated me by sponsoring a professional wrestling competition. The company manufactures 'W-front' shorts for men and it was thought that the competition (with TV coverage) would prove a valuable advertising medium. Now I loathe professional wrestling with its phoney fouls and mimed violence, so I wrote a stinging letter to the company's chairman and presented my shares to the McWhirter Cleaner Sex Foundation.

These moves backfired. The Foundation accepted the shares, but promptly sold them to the UPW (Union of Professional Wrestlers), and the competition proved an enormous success, sparked off fantastic sales of 'W-fronts' and caused the shares to rocket. I had inadvertently subsidised wrestling and thrown away a smallish fortune.

'Tell me about the days when Britain, too, was a developing country.'

On another occasion I objected strongly when it came to my ears that International Barium, a company in which I held some 200 non-voting ordinary shares, was contributing handsomely to the fighting fund of the Conservative party. I wrote a stiff letter to all the leading papers, pointing out that, while I had no interest in politics, I thought it scandalous that shareholders' money should be used in support of sectional interests.

The letter struck home and within a week the chairman of International Barium had announced that he accepted my strictures, was making reparation by giving additional and identical sums to both the Labour and Liberal parties and as a result was compelled to reduce the final dividend per share from 2½p to 2p. Another dismal failure for me.

In 1968 a company called Mompax Utilities got into hot water when the Ministry of Health accused it of polluting the Thames with noxious factory effluents. I was horrified and badly wanted to make some personal gesture that would embarrass the Mompax people, but because I had no connection with the company, owned none of its shares and used none of its products I felt uninvolved and weaponless. There seemed only one thing to do: I bought a stake in the company with the sole purpose of ridding myself of it and creating a stink in the process.

But a queer thing happened. Mompax decided that they could not rejig their production to conform with the factory acts and health regulations and would therefore close down. The shares became valueless overnight and I had invested something like £500 to no purpose.

Then take the case of Fensley Securities, a company that specialises in asset-stripping and has thrown many thousands of workers on the scrapheap by zealous rationalisation. Early in 1970, when Fensley shares stood at 23p, I read an article in one of the financial weeklies about the Fensley boss, Cary Le Mayer, a young Old Etonian with the Midas touch and a heart of iron. It seemed to me that Le Mayer was worth backing if he could be persuaded to adopt a more reasonable attitude to the worker and to go easy on the redundancies.

So before committing myself to the shares I craved an interview with the young financial wizard and entertained him to lunch at the Gargoyle.

'You wanna make plenty bread, dad?' he said, sipping his cognac.

Startled, I bit through my cigar before answering.

'Well, yes, of course,' I said, 'but not at the expense of men's jobs. I'm sure you're clever enough to make a lot of money without causing unnecessary suffering.'

'Mebbe there's some other way,' said Le Mayer, 'but I dig it not.'

And he went on to explain that he was performing an invaluable service to the British economy by hunting out under-used assets, closing down inefficient production units and selling off chunks of property and industrial potential to people with new ideas.

I still didn't like the set-up, but the shares were zooming so I decided to get aboard and hold on to my hat. I sold everything, car, house, bat and pads and bought Fensleys at 31p.

As I write the shares stand at 976p and seem to rocket with every appalling increase in the unemployment figures.

Ashamed? Of course I am. I can't think how I let myself get involved. And I don't know what to do to be saved. I can't sell out without making enormous profits and feeling unclean, so I suppose I shall have to sit tight and wait for Le Mayer to grow old and develop a conscience. Only then will the shares lose their shine.

The worry of it all has made me unfit for work and I now live (in one or other of my five new estates) by selling off a handful of my Fensley Securities every few months. Only a few though. Just enough to pay the staff and the Harrods account and to keep the cars, the yacht and my private aircraft in good going order.

Meanwhile the shares go up and up inexorably. Let my plight be a lesson to the imprudent investor. The worst day's work I ever did was to take Cary Le Mayer to lunch at the Gargoyle and to fall under his evil spell, and my only consolation is the knowledge that I am now, like the thousand of workers affected by Le Mayer's machinations, unemployed.

ANNUAL REPORTS, THINGS OF BEAUTY

For some years now I have been acutely embarrassed by certain aspects of my post or mail. I am a very small, dwarf investor and the companies in which I hold derisively minimal stakes insist on treating me as if I were a Clore, a Slater or a Getty. Every year without fail they send me sumptuously produced volumes entitled *Report and Accounts* which are certainly worth more as works of art, or in terms of glossy paper, Cellophane and colour reproductions, than the market value of my share of the equity.

Take last year's *Report and Accounts* of Mimrod Holdings. It was too big to go through the letter-box and was handed to me by an underpaid postman who happens to be one of the liveliest seam-up bowlers in village cricket. The volume, contained in a cardboard case, consisted of ninety pages of facts and figures interlarded with superb colour photographs of the chairman, the entire staff of Grimblestone (a subsidiary), the head offices of eighty associated companies in various parts of the world, and 73 products ranging from buses to bottles and ball-points, together with maps and a pull-out chart showing how the holding company, its subsidiaries and associates are managed.

I spent the whole morning leafing through the book, studying the amazing pictures and tearing out the sheets of transparent plastic (made from imported oil) for my wife's use in the kitchen. Then after lunch I wrote as follows to Sir Marcus Slaverly, the chairman:

Dear Sir, I am much impressed by the format, texture and material content of the annual Report and Accounts which you were good enough to send me, and without in any way wishing to teach my grandmother, etc., I should like to make a few observations and recommendations.

1. Is it sensible to treat all shareholders alike? I know we are a democracy and all that, but it seems crazy and shockingly wasteful to equate me with my 10 shares in Mimrod with someone like K.V. Slaughtered who in 1973 according to the R & A held 2,017,530 'beneficial interests' in the company. Mr Slaughtered seems to be *entitled* to a hardback edition of the Report, while I should be quite satisfied with a mimeographed sheet listing the barest details of the financial position. Indeed, since you usually take a half-page in all the quality dailies to publish a potted version of the Report I don't really see why you should bother with me at all.

2. A trivial and somewhat delicate matter. For the last seven

years the frontispiece of the Report has taken the form of a portrait of your good self. The first of the series, by the distinguished artist Terence Cuneo (I think), was excellent. I liked the Churchillian pose; the determined expression and the way your watch chain ('gastric jewellery' as H.G. Wells called it, referring to Arnold Bennett's waistcoat display) echoed the curve of your second chin. But in subsequent years this gem of portraiture has been replaced by the works of artists of the *avant garde* school with which I do not sympathise. Last year's study, giving you two eyes on the same side of your nose, struck me as being derivative and unpleasant.

However, my chief complaint concerns the repetitious nature of the subject matter of these portraits. In these days of difficult industrial relations wouldn't it be helpful to vary the frontispiece by depicting other members of the Mimrod organisation? Pictures of senior shop stewards, Stakhanovite workers, pretty secretaries or PROs would make a change and, I believe, encourage employees.

'*Well, I suppose the smaller oil sheikhs have to put their money somewhere.*'

3. My chief point. Can the company afford this sumptuary expenditure? There are 2,500,000-odd shareholders throughout the world and if you produce and dispatch this number of Reports the cost must be staggering. The postage of my copy was 45p: what does it cost to get copies to shareholders in America, Australia and Hong Kong? The mind boggles! My own rough estimate of total expenditure on the project works out at £6 million, and this doesn't include the fees of the advertising agency that commissioned the editing, design and printing of the opus.

Now £6 million may not seem much these days, but only the other day I read that you are experiencing cash flow difficulties.

There must be many shareholders who, like me, would prefer an increase in dividend to a post Report and Accounts.

Hoping that you will accept these comments in the constructive spirit in which they are made, I remain, yours faithfully, Bernard Hollowood.

A week later I received the following communication:

Dear Mr Hollinshead, The Deputy Chairman has asked me to reply to your courteous letter of June 3.

The annual *Report and Accounts* is an important document and deserves, we feel, to be given expert presentation. Mimrod has many rivals among the multinationals and conglomerates and we cannot afford to let them steal a march on us propagandawise. Moreover the Chairman, Sir Marcus Slaverley, is dead keen on the Business Accounts Competition organised by the *Sunday Globe*. We were runners-up to Skivex International in 1971, came fourth in 1972 and received an 'honourable mention' last year.

You will, we know, be pleased to know that Sir Marcus has high hopes of carrying off the first prize of a month in Bermuda and a replica of the *Sunday Globe* trophy for this year's *Report and Accounts*.

Yours in sisterhood, Molly Pshawn (Ms), secretary to Mr Mason Burbank, assistant to the Deputy Chairman.

(Dictated by Molly Pshawn (Ms) and signed in her absence by Dolores Clam.)

CAN ASTROLOGY HELP YOUR PORTFOLIO?

AT A PARTY a few months ago a woman who ought to know better came up to me and said: 'I've been watching you and I've decided that you must be a Gem.'

'Well, thanks,' I said, 'but I doubt whether my wife would agree with you.'

'You see,' she said, 'you're like me. Geminis don't like olives in martinis.'

'Oh, that kind of gem,' I said. 'I'm afraid I've no idea what I am, and I regard astrology as bunk.'

'Then you're very stupid,' she said. 'Were you born between May 22 and June 21?'

'June 3,' I said. 'What of it?'

'I was right. You are a Gemini, and Geminis are entering a phase of staggering opportunity. Do you invest?'

'Well,' I said. 'I dabble occasionally. Nothing serious, though.'

'Then if you take the advice of your horoscope you'll make a mint of money before April 6.'

'Let me get you another drink,' I said, and made my escape into the throng.

The next morning over breakfast I was riffling through the *Gazette* in quest of a soccer report when my eye lit on a column headed 'The Stars and You,' and I was instantly reminded of the woman with the dyed hair and carmine fingernails. The stupid bitch! What was it she'd called me? A Gem. I glanced at the column and the word Gemini seemed to pulsate like an electric advertisement.

'Marvellous opportunities present themselves,' it read. 'The letters of your name are the keys to financial success, but only if you are bold. Be cautious though about a rendezvous in the evening and prepare for a longish journey.'

Piffle! Absolute rubbish! It seems they'll do anything these days to sell newspapers.

I was dining that evening at the Casablanca with an old friend, male, and as I made my way there after a late session at the office I laughed at the recollected warning about my rendezvous. Silas had booked a table and was waiting for me with martinis at the ready. But before I could sit down a hand with long carmine nails clutched my arm.

'Hellow, fellow Gem,' she said. 'I hope you took my advice.'

Then she resumed her seat at the next table, and throughout the meal I was conscious of her presence. Perhaps I *should* have been more cautious about the rendezvous.

'Well, how about it?' said Silas. 'Are you game?'

It was acutely embarrassing. I had not been listening, and I had to admit as much.

Silas never allows himself to be nettled. He grinned.

'Something on your mind?' he said. 'A woman?'

'Could be,' I said, and then I heard him repeat his offer of a free flight to Kingston, Jamaica, to see a Test match, West Indies versus Australia. And, of course, I snapped his hand off. He'd bought the tickets months before, planning the trip as a wedding anniversary treat for his wife, but Mrs Silas had cried off to look after an ailing parent.

'Terrific,' I said. 'I've always wanted to see the West Indies perform on their own wickets.'

And as I said it I noticed that the woman at the next table was nodding her head approvingly.

'It's odd,' I said. 'By chance I looked at one of those astrology columns this morning and it told me to prepare for a longish journey.'

Silas hooted. 'Oh, no,' he said, 'not *you*! Don't tell me that the great sceptic himself has been hooked on that tommy-rot!'

'Of course not,' I said. 'It's just a remarkable coincidence.'

After dinner we walked across to my club for a nightcap and bumped into Reggie Crawshaw. Reggie had clearly been knocking them back. He was more than usually loquacious and bursting with news.

'I'm in the money,' he said. 'Or shall be soon. Had lunch with . . . (and here he mentioned a notorious financial whiz-kid) 'and got the lowdown on what's cooking in the City straight from the horse's mouth.'

'Oh, yeah,' said Silas.

'He's plunging for Berensons Holdings in a big way. And Evans Electrics, Rugby Portland Cement, Nidas Chemicals, Armitage Motors . . . Why don't you chaps get aboard?'

I'm too old a hand to follow the crowd in the investment game merely on the strength of a verbal say-so, but when I got home and thought over the evening's conversation I was galvanised into immediate action by an astonishing discovery.

Reggie's tips were for Berensons, Evans, Rugby, Nidas and Armitage, the initial letters of which spelled BERNA, and my Christian name is – well, to spare my blushes consult the heading of this article. 'The Stars and You' had said: 'The Letters of your name are the keys to financial success.' Incredible. Another coincidence? Or was there something in astrology after all?

Next morning I got in touch with my broker, sold most of my blue chip industrials and bought £300-worth of each of Reggie's recommended shares.

For a week my acquisitions improved slightly and I bought copies of Zarathustra's *Horoscopes Translated*, Ben Khan's *In Our Stars* and Klatinka's *Astrological Man*. Then, quite suddenly, all five of my new investments nosedived.

There's no fool like an old fool. Sick at heart, I burned my astrology collection and, as an act of penance, put myself on a non-smoking, non-alcoholic, vegetarian diet.

And because I was off the booze I avoided my old haunts and saw nothing of my friends – for a matter of six weeks. Then, one evening I bumped into Reggie Crawshaw in the Strand.

'Did you make a packet on Ranelagh and Dupont?' he said, after patting me on the back.

'Ranelagh and Dupont?' I said. 'No, but I lost a packet on the shares you *did* tip. Thanks very much – for nothing!'

'But Ranelagh has rocketed and Dupont have trebled in value since I gave you the nod! I know I let you in because Silas Whatsisname rang me up only last night to thank me. He's made a cool thou.'

Had I really shut my ears to Reggie's two winners? Or had I heard them and quickly forgotten them? It was sickening – especially so when it suddenly dawned on me that Ranelagh and Dupont would have supplied the 'R' and 'D' to complete my name.

Mind you, I still think astrology is for the birds.

A FACE-LIFT FOR MON REPOS

ONE OF the safest ways of saving these days is to put your money into home improvement. During the enormous surge in property prices of recent years many people have made a *business* of house improvement – taking over and inhabiting one run-down establishment after another and converting it into a desirable, marketable and profitable residence by the addition of mod cons and attractive extensions.

I am not recommending home improvement on this scale to people who like a bit of peace and quiet. To be permanently surrounded by builders, plasterers, plumbers and electricians and to sleep night after night with one's head against a wall of flapping tarpaulin is my idea of hell. But such discomforts can be tolerated if their duration is relatively brief and if they can be given a cash value, or rather a capital value, of thousands of pounds.

Home improvement is not, however, merely a matter of converting the loft into a smart study-bedroom and adding a second bath and loo. No, it is an enterprise calling for immense flair and/or low cunning. First you must improve the property's status by giving it what the agents call 'a good address.' A farm labourer's cottage known as 'No 3 The Cottages,' 'Afore Ye Go,' 'The Nook,' 'Mon Repos,' 'Highbury' or 'Stamford Bridge' can be given a face-lift worth roughly £1,000 by the addition merely of a new name-plate marked 'The Old Vicarage,' 'Manor House Farm,' 'St. Bede's Lodge,' 'The Maltings' or 'Franklyn Castle.' Critics who object that such changes are inaccurate, misleading or highfalutin should be told that the house has been named after a ship: owners of dinghies think nothing of dubbing their craft 'Casablanca,' 'Buck House,' 'Windsor Castle' or 'The Taj Mahal.'

The next job is to write a description of your ideal house and then doctor your premises to live up to it. To convert a very ordinary 3-bedroomed house into 'Immaculate, fully-heated, 5-bedroom, 3 bath, double-glazing, patio, garage. Within range of sea. Developed garden' all you need are a couple of second-hand zinc baths (portable), a few square yards of plywood partitioning, an Elsan garden privy, a bit of glass and the catalogue of a home extension contractor.

The latter will offer you all manner of ready-to-erect loggias, patios, sun lounges, etc., but you need buy only a second-hand greenhouse and place this just outside your front door. Conservatory, patio, loggia or rumpus-room – call it what you will – you have now put another £3,000 on the value of the house.

I am not too keen on loft conversions. My experience of life in an attic – in my student days – left me round-shouldered and suffering from head noises. The contours of the apartment were such that I could stand upright without banging my head only when equidistant from the front and rear walls which were of course linked by a roof shaped like an inverted 'V.' My constant companion in these cramped quarters was the main cistern, equipped with a ball-cock that creaked in every joint, and I pored over my books to a cacophony of water music.

Another disadvantage of this bed-sitter, or bed-stooper, was that entrance to it was via a ladder from the bathroom, so that my movements were dictated by the landlady's ablutions. I might be trapped in my room while the family took it in turn to bathe or I might be encouraged to help Mr Travis with his gardening while Mrs Travis, washing her hair, barred me from the ladder and my books.

On the other hand there is much to be said for garage, garden shed and out-house conversions. If you are lucky enough – like a friend of mine – to have a garage that is situated 20 or 30 yards from the house it might be possible to get local authority permission to improve it. My friend invited the authority to inspect the building after he'd spent an hour or two undermining the structure's stability and making sure that its roof leaked, and then, with permission granted, called in an architect to design a sumptuous garage, capacity half a dozen cars, beneath a roomy flat equipped with all mod cons, a studio, kitchen and glazed balcony.

'Stock Exchange? Certainly – straight on past Kuwait Point, left at the Iran complex, left again at Saudi Arabia House and you'll see the SE right next to Bahrain Buildings.'

This noble edifice cost him £10,500, and a few months after completion of the fiddle he moved in with his wife and dog and sold his garage-less house for £18,750 to a brother-in-law.

The advertising of your reconstituted desirable residence is a job for experts. It is so easy to spoil a glowing encomium with a careless word or two. For example, if you mention 'double garage' among the features of your £28,990 bargain, it is a mistake to add 'near main bus route' or 'convenient bus stop.' By all means air your views about the certainty of increasing petrol prices and the need to replace the private car by improved public transport, but try to be consistent and don't mention the convenient bus stop unless you alter that 'double garage' to 'extensive outhouse suitable for stable, potting-shed or billiards room.'

Similarly I should play down your 'extra-large heated swimming pool.' Yes, it was heavenly during that hot spell last June, but you know as well as I do that with fuel and water and labour as scarce as they are every dip you take in 1974 is likely to set you back getting on for £62.50. People who read house ads are not fools and they are fully aware of what happens to one-tenth of an acre of water that's left untended, unfiltered and uncared for.

If you mention this white elephant at all your best line would be something like 'Extensive garden offers facilities for splendid winter skating' or 'Large sunken container for reserve coal stocks.'

The chief snag about house improvement is that it's so popular. You do up your present house for £3,000 or £4,000 and hope to flog it for £23,000 and buy a smaller place for, say, £18,000; but you discover that every smallish house worth looking at has been converted and extended by its present owners and is now on offer at £30,000. I should know.

I mean, what chance have I got of finding a 'pleasant country house, restructured to economy size by the *removal* of one wing, two bathrooms, one tennis court and one garage, and by the filling-in of attractive swim-pool to form established shrubbery?' None. None at all. And, heaven knows, I've looked hard enough.

SEVEN-POINT PLAN TO BEAT THE BLUES

I WANT to offer words of avuncular comfort to readers who have steadfastly refused to panic in the current recession, and intend to stick with their sickly equities. Yes, you there with the boiled egg, who can't find anything more to read in the sports pages.

You are like me. You have a few shares and you remained faithful to them as they fluttered down in 1973. In December you could stand it no longer, but you still didn't sell; you decided to stick your head in the sand, ignore the stock market prices in the paper and switch off the news before the reader could announce the sorry state of the FT index.

We are the unflappable core of the British public. We know that some of the clever investors went liquid six months ago, are now getting 14 p.c. interest on their money from the Rossingley Rural District Water Board, and are hovering like vultures over the market, waiting to pounce as soon as shares show signs of recovery. And there are times when we envy these febrile creatures. But not for long. At any moment we can comfort ourselves with the knowledge that we have, in a way *already* pounced. Not for us the awful problem of when to get back into the market: we're in there already, the pioneers of the next boom.

Of course there are pundits who try to scare us into belated activity. You know who I mean – *'The market has a long way to go before it bottoms out,' 'I expect a floor of 200 towards the end of '74'* and *'Don't be deceived by technical adjustments: the trend is still downwards'* – I mean the writers of this kind of garbage.

And even more worrying are the economists who tell us that this is not an ordinary slump, but the end of equities as a hedge against inflation. 'We've seen this coming for years,' they say. 'For at least a decade the market has lived on phoney values and at last the bubble of credibility has been pricked. Shares can never return to the levels of 1972.' Well, we've heard all that before. In 1970 shares were never again going to recapture their glitter of 1968, and in 1966 they couldn't recover their 1964 values, and in 1962 . . . Yes, some of us can go back quite a few years with the Jeremiahs.

But the market is still terribly depressing and you need all the help you can get. So I thought I'd tell you how I personally have coped with the blues. Here is a list of things you can do to remain sane and cheerful and, at the very least, abandon thoughts of suicide.

1. Attribute your market inactivity to indolence. Adopt a couldn't-care-less attitude and when friends ask whether you have sold your shares yet, look bored and say, *'Too much trouble, old boy. I've gone into hibernation until '75.'*

2. When you *do* allow yourself to check up on share prices, multiply each figure by 2.4 to allow for decimalisation. A share that has slumped to (say) a sickening 97 can look quite respectable when seen as 223.2 old pence. Similarly, when you envy the high interest rates being pocketed by the liquid brigade, remember to translate their take-home divi (after deduction of income tax and surtax) into *real* purchasing power. Interest of 14 p.c. on £100 invested in Farrowsby Council bonds will enable cleversticks to buy the leg of one pair of trousers per annum. If that.

3. Remember that you bought your shares as a long-term investment, and that your original idea of a long term should be extended with the increase in life-expectancy. Your plan to retire on the proceeds of your investment capital is a non-starter anyway. What's the use of retiring when there's not enough petrol to get to the golf club? Do you really want to be stuck in one room, round one electric bar, with the rest of the family? Wouldn't you miss the coy camaraderie of the office by candlelight? Put off your retirement date for five years to allow for economic recovery, influx of North Sea oil, the smashing success of Concorde, etc., and give your shares another five years to reach a satisfactory selling price.

4. Trot along to the public library and grab as many books as possible about the great American crash of 1929. Read them diligently until you know what a *real* slump is like, and count your blessings.

5. If the procedure in (1) above does not appeal to your temperament, try adopting the swagger of the out-and-out speculator. I have just been reading a book which states that to

hang on to shares in a falling market is reckless gambling. It could be, therefore, that instead of the unadventurous, stoical and somewhat stuffy investor you thought you were, you are in fact a devil-may-care dashing, casino-like speculator. Live up to the part. Cultivate a thin moustache and go in for loud suits and opulent cufflinks. Become something of a gay dog at the office and be seen squiring the blonde from the typing pool at the greyhound track and a smart discotheque. In other words, make the most of your newly-discovered reputation.

6. If your wife accuses you of cowardice because you no longer study the share prices, tell her that the small print is bad for your eyes. If she then says she will read out the prices for you, complain about the acoustics of the sitting-room and reveal that your hearing is not quite what it was. When she offers to chalk up the prices in jumbo-sized figures remind her that you had to give up night school years ago because chalk-dust seemed to bring on attacks of asthma.

7. Finally, decide to sell only if the FT index dips to some such improbable figure as 53. This gives you about 250 points to play with, as it were, and absolves you from any further worry about your shares. Forget all about them and take up some enthralling hobby (stamp collecting, property-development, 18th century porcelain or ballroom dancing) to keep your mind active.

I do hope I have been able to help. If not write to Uncle Bernard with your *personal* problem and enclose s.a.e. and a money order for £500.

PART 2
ECONOMICS MOSTLY

WHY MANAGERS LACK CHARISMA

IN THE City pages recently Arnold Weinstock, boss of GEC, made the startling confession 'I am just a manager . . ' Now Mr Weinstock, the son of an immigrant Polish tailor, was educated at the London School of Economics, Cambridge University and the Admiralty, and it is odd to find him with the semblance of a chip on his shoulder.

Then Lord Kearton, who was lucky enough to be at school with the writer of this article, and went on to Oxford, told Robert McKenzie in a TV programme 'I am only an industrialist.'

Lord Kearton went further in self criticism, dismissed his life peerage as of 'little consequence nowadays,' and admitted to a relatively low position in the social pecking order. And in doing so I think he put his finger on *the* English disease.

'I know it's a lot of money, lady, but you must remember that our sausages contain a high proportion of very expensive bread.'

Managers and industrialists have nothing like the social esteem in Britain that they enjoy overseas. For centuries our top people have been the landed gentry, and even in the so-called egalitarian 'seventies it is the rule rather than the exception for successful young City tycoons to acquire large estates and try to forget how they made their money.

When industrialists are slighted it is because they thrive on profit, for profit is still seen by the majoirty as the usurer's 'turn,' money neither worked for nor inherited, the bonus granted to the few by the capitalist system. That workers should hold such views is natural enough: to them profits are seen quite naturally as undistributed wages.

But the profit motive is also suspect in the eyes of many salaried and rentier types, and I am pretty certain that a referendum on the question 'Is profit-making an entirely desirable economic goal?' would get less than majority approval.

The apologists tell us that profit is the reward for risking capital, that profits represent a company's savings rather than a fountain of dividends. They would even go so far – most of them – as to claim that profit is the life-blood of industry and commerce and that all productive activity would cease if profits were to be appropriated or made illegal.

This is true only under conditions of competitive private enterprise: beyond the Iron Curtain, where dividends are unknown, the USSR somehow manages to rustle up the millions of roubles needed by an advanced technology, for space probes, nuclear submarines, the upkeep of the Kremlin and expense account vodka and caviar.

Because I happen to think the British system preferable, I feel it my duty to outline a policy for the successful reform of our class system.

1. Industrialists should be extremely chary about appearing on TV. At present they can be roped in at a moment's notice and are therefore seen by the public as *performers*, artists who are neither funny in the Max Wall, Morecambe and Wise way, nor as attractive as our sporting personalities and show-biz idols. Industrialists are often confused on the box with politicians or weather forecasters and thus they lack charisma. We still look up to and touch the forelock at Dukes and other dignitaries who *never* offer themselves for inspection via the little screen.

If Lord Kearton, Lord Goodman and Sir Fred Catherwood absented themselves from the box a year or two, they would rush up the ladder of social prestige and never again confess to being *only* an industrialist or *just* a manager.

2. Because good industrial relations are essential to profitable production, bosses have to get on with their underlings, know most of their senior white-collar-workers by sight and remember the Christian names of at least half a dozen of their thousands of wage-earning employees. Not an easy task.

Sir Harry Lampblack, I remember, got round this latter problem by instructing his personnel officer to recruit foremen only if they were called William. Then Sir Harry could breeze through the works scattering 'Morning, William,' 'Everything OK, Bill?' and 'How's tricks, Willie?' without making a mistake. He earned the undying affection of his workers.

Unfortunately, the practice of talking face to face with all and sundry tends to have a deleterious effect on a boss's accent. He slips into the local lingo and forgets all those little tricks of pronunciation which differentiate industrialists and landed gentry.

Thus he may find himself saying 'at home' when he really means 'a tome,' saying 'temporary' instead of 'tempry,' 'secretary' for 'secetry,' and 'etcetra' for 'ecsetra.' And if he lets himself go like this, is it any wonder that his invitation to the hunt ball should go mysteriously astray in the post year after year?

The successful boss is truly bilingual. By all means let him adopt the native speech of the peasants in the office, foundry, packing shed and canteen, but his secretary, however inefficient, must be in Debrett and keep his vowels in order.

3. Finally, we come to the boss's address. Ideally his country seat should lie amid at least 2,000 acres of which half are woodland, threaded with trout streams. He should be seen in the village every other week riding a mettlesome mare, and once a month he should stand 'drinks all round' for the customers of the 'Dog and Partridge.'

His wife will prefer doing her own housework, but there should be a cast of 'Upstairs, Downstairs' proportions to be included in 'family' photographs.

I hope this helps. Of course the whole social set-up could change very rapidly with a prolonged stock market boom. Land, and the gentry that go with it, acquire inflated values when the FT index is sagging.

When the index hits 550 again, as it must, the industrialist will once more achieve social pre-eminence, and I shall be commenting on the sad case of the Marquis who moaned: 'Of course, I am only a landowner.'

DO YOU HAVE A NO.3 ACCOUNT?

AS I remember them, the banks of my youth were invariably empty of customers. I would saunter into the Whitehall & City Bank (Coketown branch) and immediately experience a frisson of nervousness as I breathed air chilled by expanses of marble and polished mahogany. A clerk, male, would be waiting to serve me and address me as 'sir.' I used to whisper as if in church.

I now visit the bank about once a month and always I have to queue for service behind a man collecting wages for a multinational company, a schoolmistress depositing dinner money collected during the week from upwards of 500 children, and a man paying in the month's takings of about 20 one-armed bandits located in the town's pubs. You'd think, wouldn't you, that the bank would operate two counters, one for business customers, one for private accounts. But no. I am kept waiting for ten minutes at least while sacks of cash are decanted and coin of the realm is stacked into leaning towers of pounds.

And the din! People seem to have no respect these days, they chatter as they would in a betting shop. Women gossip and scold their children, and men – some straight off the farm, some in overalls – treat the place as they would a locker room of a golf club. No awe.

I have never quite recovered from the embarrassment occasioned by my first borrowing from a bank. The sum involved was £100, and I needed it to complete the cash purchase of a house costing £500. Yes, £500. It wasn't much of a house, and without the support of the buildings on its flanks it would probably have subsided into a puff of rubble and dust, but it was all I could afford.

The manager was delighted to be of service. He offered me a cigarette and we chatted about local sport. Then, after casually mentioning that interest would be payable at 5 p.c. on the amount of the loan outstanding, he said: 'Got your car outside? We're supposed to value property offered as security. Just take a quick gander.'

'I don't have a car,' I said, and he looked surprised and a little worried.

'Then we'll go in mine. Shouldn't take a jiffy to get to Meadow Terrace.'

So I climbed into his Rover and we set off. I was now feeling distinctly uncomfortable. Would No. 23 still be standing when we reached it? Would the manager be horrified by the squalid sandwich of brickwork and change his mind about the loan?

'Ah, here we are!' he said, as we approached the terrace at about 40 mph. 'Which is the one? Just point it out. No need to stop.'

'That's it,' I said, waving at a much more imposing structure at the end of the terrace, and I could have bitten off my tongue and immersed my right arm in boiling fat.

'Quite a nice place,' said the manager. 'I'd say you've got a bargain there.'

I still blush at the thought of my duplicity. I paid off the loan within a fortnight, severed my relations with the Whitehall and opened an account at the Central and Metropolitan.

Ten years later when I was working in London I received a cheque for £15 from a national newspaper for an article on 'Dr Schacht and the Nazi Economic Menace.' The cheque impressed me. Beneath the name of the newspaper was printed the mysterious sign 'No 3 Account.' This seemed to me to carry enormous weight. A company with *three* banking accounts (there might even be five or six!) was obviously well-heeled. I happened to be a youngish man who was anxious to impress, so in next to no time I was round at the Central and Metropolitan.

The manager was not too co-operative and pointed out that to divide a current account in credit on average to the tune of about £17.50 into 'A,' 'B' and 'C' accounts would prove somewhat expensive in terms of bank charges. However, I persevered and when I left I had managed to get two accounts called 'Educational Deposit' and 'Holiday Deposit,' the first to hoard money for the education of planned children and the second to finance our (my wife's and my) annual week at Paignton. Subsequently, I opened other deposit accounts labelled 'Electronics,' 'Automotive' and 'Tax Reserve,' the objects of which were the purchase of a TV set and a car and the avoidance of indebtedness to HM Commissioners. But I was never able to sign a cheque bearing the magic message 'No. 3 Account.'

All this past history does no more than set the scene for an exciting venture which should *reduce* the number of deposit accounts with the Big Four by at least a dozen.

We were chatting in the bar parlour of the Grapes the other day when Elliott began to inveigh against politicians. Elliott, like most of us, had been given a nasty fright by the stock market's long dive, so he has pulled out of his unit trusts and has gone liquid. That is, he prefers to keep his capital on deposit at the bank until, as he puts it, he 'can see which way the cookie crumbles.'

Hollowood

'If you ask me, they only admitted us to the Stock Exchange because everybody else was getting out.'

He has upwards of £2,500 invested with Barclay's, and the Government prohibits the bank from paying him more than 9½ p.c. interest on this sum, whereas depositors worth more than £10,000 can get 10½ p.c. or more on their money.

'It's disgusting! said Crabtree. 'One law for the rich, another for the poor. I've got £970-odd on deposit with the National Westminster and I think I'm getting a mere 9 per cent.'

It was then that Chivers had his bright idea.

'Suppose we pooled our resources and were able to deposit more than £10,000 co-operatively!' he said. 'We'd be quids in. They'd have to give us at least 11 p.c.'

We got the message pretty quickly, and by rounding up another half-dozen customers of the Grapes, were able to amass a notional deposit of £13,272.

The plan has not yet been put into effect. We all realise that the sum will have to be banked in one name (otherwise it would almost certainly be declared illegal), and we have not yet been able to decide which of us should have the honour.

It is not only that we distrust gentlemen's agreements: there is the awkward business of dividing up the liability to income tax and surtax on the total interest.

At the moment it looks rather as though Hentrick will get the vote, but some of us doubt whether poor old Hentrick is lame enough to be trusted. As Elliott says: 'Invalid cars aren't particularly fast, but a chap like Hentrick could be down to Folkestone and across the Channel in his three-wheeler before we could say Clarence Hatry or Horatio Bottomley.'

SECRETS OF A BUSINESS SCHOOL

YOU DIAL the number of a well-known company and ask to speak to Jack Defoe, who has been known to accept last-minute invitations to make up the village cricket eleven. The receptionist hunts through a list of extension numbers and says she's sorry but there's no one called Vaux on the premises. No, nor De Vaux. So you spell out Jack's surname and she says in a slightly hurt voice, 'You mean Mr *Defoe*! Hold on, please, and I'll see if he's there.'

While you are waiting your mind races through other possible cricketers and, sure enough, when the receptionist speaks you know that your quest is by no means at an end.

'He's away on a course,' she says.

'D'you know when he'll be back?' you say, clutching at the mad hope that Jack will return that very evening and be prepared to turn out for Megthorpe on the morrow.

'Shouldn't think he'll be back until after Christmas,' she says 'these business courses usually last six months or so.'

The business course, at somewhere like the Manchester Business School, the Henley Administrative Staff College or some lesser institution, has grown in popularity in Britain over the past decade. Chairmen and managing directors, urged by successive governments to go all out for growth and efficiency, have discovered that their executive assistants have not necessarily acquired business acumen with their Oxbridge degree in pre-Chaucerian poetry, experimental physics or oceanography. After the Hitler War America's fantastic industrial success was attributed to the alumni of the Harvard Business School (founded 1908), and in Britain, only 40 years behind the times, all manner of people quickly set up all manner of business schools and colleges and charged stiff rates for admission.

My friend, Colin Restler, thought himself unlucky. His boss sent him about four years ago to the Archduke College of Industrial Management, housed in the converted stables of a stately home in Buckinghamshire. Restler has taken a BA in textiles at Bradford, but he was unable to make head or tail of a balance sheet or an ordinary profit and loss account, hadn't a clue about critical path analysis, and thought industrial relations were what happened in a bordello.

The Archduke C of IM is run by an ex-PRO, ex-advertising account executive, ex-property bond salesman who has a string of bogus degrees bought from various establishments in America. This man, Twitt (for that is his name, believe it or not) charges £2,000 for a course lasting ten weeks inclusive of a fortnight's recuperative holiday, and such is Twitt's capacity for successful self-advertisement that British companies queue for the questionable benefit of parting with three or four executives and £6,000 or £8,000 every collegiate session.

Colin Restler is bitterly critical of Twitt and the Archduke. He maintains that the staff remain nincompoops to a man, that the lectures were boring and irrelevant, that apart from the 'Socialising Seminar,' where the secrets of desk control, Martini mixing and secretary cowing were imparted, the only valuable information provided was a glossary of jargon. This had to be learned by heart by the end of the half-term holiday. Examples:

Interdepartmental Symbiosis – occasional chat between production and packaging.

Conceptual Framework – rough or first draft of a memo.

Ongoing Conf. with SS – meeting at which conferees send out for smoked salmon sandwiches.

Infra-red – code sign for fellow traveller or someone not to be trusted.

Macrodiagnosis – taking a first look at a problem.

Microwave (verb) – to get down to brass tacks or the nitty-gritty.

Throughfallshrinkage – raw material or finished goods unaccounted for at stocktaking.

Restler tried to get Twitt to explain double-entry book-keeping, but it soon became obvious that neither the principal nor his staff had the vaguest notion of elementary accountancy.

I said that Restler considered himself unlucky, but as it turned out the course proved the making of him. On his return to Truscott's Cavalry Twill, Stockport, he was treated with a new deference by old Truscott, the chairman, and achieved rapid promotion. Since he had acquired nothing at the Archduke but a command of jargon he felt in honour bound to trot the stuff out, and was immediately regarded as a superman by all and sundry. Puzzled, Restler tried to analyse the jargon and took an evening course in English at the local poly. He read widely and discovered the beauty of Chaucer, Shakespeare, Keats, Rupert Brooke, Hardy, Shaw and so on. And as he did so he unaccountably lost his command of business jargon and began to talk, write and dictate in the King's English.

One day old Truscott breezed into Restler's office mouthing one of his favourite chunks of gobbledegook.

'We ought,' he said, 'to do a macrodiagnosis of the Latin American market with our industrial design outfit. Can do, Colin?'

'D'you mean talk to Bill and Frank?' said Restler, his features twisted into a hateful sneer.

'You know damn well what a macrodiagnosis is!' said Truscott. 'Are you out of your mind? I've been watching you lately and I'm beginning to think you need another course at the Archduke. I regard you as managerial timbre, by boy. You'll be chairman in three years *if* you keep your nose clean.'

'You think I need a spell of proboscis decontamination, eh?' said Restler, and with that the old man blew up.

The next day Restler resigned or, as he put it in his letter to Truscott, 'wished to terminate his employee-role' with the company . . .

That was two years ago when Restler promptly launched himself on a new career as head of a business school at Tring. The prospectus contains these words prominently displayed: 'The Tring Business School will insist on the use of good, concise, standard English at all times and will not tolerate jargon.'

So far not a single businessman has enrolled and not a single course has been given. Restler is approaching bankruptcy cheerfully and bears neither Truscott's nor the Archduke C of IM a grudge.

'On the contrary,' he says. 'I'm eternally grateful to them for introducing me – admittedly in a roundabout way – to the glories of English literature. And I'm not unduly pessimistic about Britain's economic future. Our decline began when we imported lousy jargon from America, and our recovery will date from the moment that we reject the muck and get back to comprehensible English.'

'And when will that be?' I asked.

'Oh, about 1984, I imagine,' he said.

WHO PAYS FOR A WEALTH TAX ?

EVERYONE who has commented so far on Labour's proposals for a wealth tax has made abundantly clear that while he holds strong views about it one way or the other the levy will not of course affect him personally. Politicians, journalists, lawyers and business men all go out of their way to plead immunity if not poverty, and can think of very few people other than the more obvious tycoons and a number of unhappy farmers who will be caught in the tax's net.

My own researches, conducted in the bar parlour of The Grapes, reveal that Mr Healey has introduced the wealth tax notion both too *early* and too *late* for it to bear fruit or satisfy the pundits.

Alec C is known to be a man of substance. He was thought to

own a fine Georgian house, two cars, a small yacht, and as pretty a second wife as any man with a gross paunch and a whisky-inflamed proboscis is entitled to. We naturally assumed that the tax would prove damaging to his bank balance . . .

'He's too late,' he said. 'Two years ago, perhaps, I might have been caught, but my portfolio has taken a frightful hammering and today I'm worth very much less than £100,000. *Very* much less. The house was worth about £50,000 before the wealth tax was mooted, but in present circumstances, I doubt whether it would fetch more than 30 and half of that belongs to my first missus.'

'He's too early,' said Jeremy T, a highly successful advertising agent. 'By the time the tax becomes law my estate will be worth nothing like £100,000. I'm making quite sure of that!'

'Don't look at *me!*' said Tom B. 'You know what schoolmasters get. If you ask me, Healey's set his sights much too high. I call a man wealthy if he's worth £20,000 including his house and colour TV.'

'Our accountant says that unless we push the boat out more we could be paying wealth tax by 1977.'

George O said that the stock market slump was a direct result of the hint of a wealth tax in Labour's 1970 manifesto. 'It took a year or two to register,' he said. 'then people with money got the wind up and decided to spend while they could. It meant getting rid of equities, and down they went. And of course it's still going on. You can't really blame people. Tax avoidance isn't a crime.'

'No,' said Henry P, a retired civil servant and an amateur ornithologist, 'but the effect of the tax, or of the threat of the tax, is decidedly unfair to ordinary people – people like me on a miserable fixed income. Both Heath and Wilson have told us that there'll be no improvement in our standard of living for two or three years, which means that there'll be no real increase in the gross national income. Right? Well, if the wealthy are going to live it up in order to reduce their liability to a wealth tax, it follows that they'll be consuming more than their normal share of the cake, and it also follows that there'll be less of the cake left for ordinary people like me. It's tragic.'

'Exactly,' said Jeremy T. 'Labour's supposed to believe in fair shares, and here they are encouraging people like me to spend money like water. Which reminds me, what'll it be? Let's make it doubles this time. It's my round and money's no object. I reckon I've got at least eighteen months to get rid of £30,000 surplus to requirements.'

He ordered eight doubles and sloughed the best part of a fiver.

Surprisingly, we eventually reached total agreement. There might be a case for a wealth tax, but it could be levied without serious damage to the fixed income brigade only during a period of boom, expansion and rising national income. We looked at the economic situation, the oil situation, the morale of British industry, and we decided that conditions *suitable* for a wealth tax were unlikely to emerge for several years. Assuming that all goes well with North Sea and Celtic Sea oil we thought 1984 might prove to be the ideal year for the tax, and 1984, we remembered, was the year of George Orwell and 'Big Brother.'

EVERY MAN HAS HIS PRICE-EVEN UMPIRES

THERE'S a move afoot to make Members of Parliament declare their financial interests. Not surprisingly, the most active campaigners are the Liberals, who are somewhat thin on the ground in Westminster, and the Socialists, most of whom don't believe in financial interests and wouldn't be chosen as parliamentary candidates if they had any. And, not surprisingly, the MPs most reluctant to reveal are the Conservatives, many of them rather well-to-do and well-connected and all of them passionately devoted to *private* enterprise and ever ready to preach the virtues of the acquisitive society.

Are MPs a special case or should all of us be required to make our financial interests public? Take the writer of this article for example. The other week, in an article, I mentioned Polygrade Graphite, the pencil manufacturers, stating that I found their 3B model eminently satisfactory for marking newspaper paragraphs destined for my scrapbook. I wrote innocently, carelessly, quite forgetting that Polygrade is a subsidiary of Benson and Cosgrave, a company in which I have a few shares.

When I realised what I had done I was horrified. I detest advertising of this kind with its ugly aroma of payola! So what did I do? My first idea was to write articles containing casual references in praise of the 3B pencils of Venus and Royal

Sovereign pencils, Polygrade's chief competitors. But almost as soon as I reached for my typewriter it dawned on me that I was being woefully insular. What about foreign pencil manufacturers! They too would suffer to some extent from my selective advocacy of Polygrade. To put matters right I would have to obtain a list of the world's pencil makers and write hundreds of articles!

The task was beyond me. Finally, I decided to put matters right in a single short story containing a vaguely disparaging reference to Polygrade's 3B, and after a lot of thought I came up with 'Seizing the first pencil to hand, a Polygrade 3B, a writing instrument in which he had less than perfect confidence, Simon dashed off a letter to his MP . . .'

That, I thought, would even things out. Unfortunately, the story has not yet been published. Three editors have rejected it and I am now converting into a 'Thirty Minute Theatre' play for the BBC. I shan't sleep properly until I have eased my conscience about Polygrade.

Many years ago while racing at Ascot I fell madly in love with Gwen, chestnut filly of about sixteen hands. My love was reciprocated and during that summer we met regularly at Ayr, Epsom, Doncaster, Thirsk, Uttoxeter and Market Rasen. One day in August I arranged to meet Gwen in London outside the building where she was employed as a secretary. I never kept the date. On the appointed day I reached the rendezvous to discover that the establishment for which she worked was the *News Chronicle*. At the time I was a free-lance contributor to that newspaper, my pseudonym appearing fairly regularly atop a column devoted to the game of draughts, and I was deeply shocked to know that I had unwittingly struck up a friendship with one of the paper's employees.

The choice before me was simple: I could either cease to contribute to the *News Chronicle* or I could put an end to my affair with Gwen. What I could not do was further my amorous liaison without declaring my financial interest in her place of employment. So the chestnut filly faded from my life and I suffered heavily for my principles: in the following year the *Chronicle* ceased publication and from that day (a Friday, I think) to this I have never written a word about draughts.

Readers may consider me over-scrupulous in my observance of business ethics, and they may well be right. Certainly my squeamishness has more than once caused me acute embarrassment and on one occasion made me a small fortune.

When I gave up active cricket I umpired for the village of Mexthorpe. One of the Mexthorpe players was a Mr Smith (not his real name) who was something in the City and rich enough to run three cars and employ a butler. Smith used his money to buy success in all his activities and it was no surprise to me when he tried to bribe his way to stardom as a bowler.

He began by offering me a fiver for every lbw decision I made in his favour, and of course I told him to go to Helvellyn. Then he tried the bait of tips on horses.

'Oh, come off it, Hollowood,' he said. 'Every man has his

price. If you'll give me the wicket of Sir Ronald in next week's derby game with Melchett Bolsover I'll give you a cert, a horse that's bound to win at 50 to one.'

There was deadly rivalry between the two teams and real animosity between Smith and Sir Ronald. Well, Mexthorpe batted first and made 98 and Melchett Bolsover were 62 for six when Sir Ronald came to the crease. Smith was bowling at my end and his first ball hit Sir Ronald's right pad smack in front.

'Owzat?' yelled Smith, and to my amazement I shook my head. During the next hour Smith appealed against Sir Ronald at least a dozen times and ten of them should have been answered in the affimative. But Smith's behaviour had maddened me and I took a perverse delight in rejecting his appeals and watching him dance with rage and frustration.

Sir Ronald made 27 not out and the winning run was a leg-bye following yet another unsuccessful appeal for lbw.

I didn't join the teams in 'The Crown' after the game: I was too upset.

But on Monday I got a strange 'thank you' letter from Sir Ronald – 'I greatly appreciated your umpiring on Saturday,' it said. 'In fact I have never in all my life experienced such skill and such integrity in an umpire. One expects partisanship from 'home' umpires, especially when they are adjudicating in local derbys, but, you, sir, leaned over backwards to be fair. Indeed, on one occasion I thought I was lucky to be given the benefit of the doubt, but the ball would, I suppose, have missed the leg stump by a whisker.

'The enclosed is a small tribute from one sportsman to another. It is little enough at today's prices, but invested in Fraser Longhouse ordinaries within the next few days it should bring you a sizeable capital gains. Yours gratefully, Ronald Longhouse.'

The cheque was for £100. A fortnight later, after the merger, it was worth almost £500. It was money acquired both honestly and dishonestly.

So I am not entirely convinced that to declare one's interests means any sacrifice of financial opportunity.

I NEED £21,850 BY 1978, OR ELSE...

UNTIL the other day I had never thought seriously of emigrating. I won't deny that the idea of belonging to the 'brain drain' has always seemed flattering and tempting to one still smarting with the disgrace of failing to pass the Oxford Schools Certificate examination at the first time of asking; but I decided long ago that to cut myself off from daily contact with the English countryside, the sports pages of the newspapers and

British radio and TV would be unmitigated folly.

The experiences of some of my friends confirmed me in this decision. In 1950, Alec B gave up his job as a schoolmaster and sailed with his family for Santiago where a lucrative post as tutor to the children of a wealthy Chilean guano merchant awaited him. Six months later he was back in England, opening the innings for his village cricket team. 'Chile was fine,' he said, 'and so was the job, but when April came round I began to panic as I realised that I should never again have a chance of scoring 1,000 runs in May. Oh, I know 27 is my highest May total to date, but you never know, do you? Anyway, out there in Santiago I couldn't get the Midthorpe village green out of my mind, so one day I bundled the family into a jumbo jet and a week later I was teaching geography again and practising my cover drive.'

'Ever since you were a baby we've paid into a fund for your public school education, but I'm sure you'll agree that the house badly needs painting both inside and out.'

Then there was Philip C, physicist, who one day in 1958 left a top research job with ICI to work for Du Pont in America for roughly three times his former take-home pay. Philip liked the States and soon adapted to ice-cold beer, centrally overheated offices and laboratories and non-stop TV commercials. But in 1959 his wife, Doreen, was mugged on her way home from a concert at Carnegie Hall and spent six months in hospital where she underwent three cosmetic operations.

Philip was able to pay the fees of the anaesthetist and surgeon by selling his home and contents and by taking a second job as projectionist in an all-nite cinema, but the hospital bills for blood, food, drugs and laundry were hopelessly beyond his means. As soon as Doreen was on her feet he settled his debts with the help of an American money-lender and returned to Britain. He pays the American the dollar equivalent of £132 a month and plans to be out of his clutches by August, 1993. His old employer would have welcomed Philip back, but Pilbeam

Pharmaceuticals of Crewe, manufacturers of 'Doglax,' the popular slimming food for dogs, secured his services by offering him a rent-free house and £15 a week more than ICI.

The case of Saul G is particularly interesting. He had struggled for twenty years to make his mark with Lofferton Engineering and by Christmas, 1973, was about to hit the jackpot with a seat on the board. Then in swift succession came the 3-day week, the General Election and the Budget, and Saul saw his access to share options, a villa in Wilmslow and a yacht nipped in the bud.

He resigned and managed almost immediately to land an excellent job in Auckland, where he and his family found the climate and the food much to their liking. Saul was reasonably thick-skinned and philosophical and being frequently addressed as a 'Pom bastard' did not worry him unduly. His wife, Mona, however, had led a sheltered life and Pom bashing shocked and distressed her. On her first shopping jaunt a female counterhand pushed a leg of lamb at her with the remark 'That'll be $2.75, you stuck-up, illegit Pommie' and a parking attendant called her a 'misbegot Pom immigrant.'

After that she refused to leave the house and Saul found life unbearable, and three months later he was back in Salford.

Not very encouraging, are they, these case-histories? Yet, after reading in the *Economist* that a man now earning £10,000 a year will probably need £40,000 by 1978 to achieve the same standard of living, my opposition to personal involvement in the brain drain has steadily been eroded. Scaling down the figures I realise with horror that unless by 1978 I have upped my earnings to the ridiculous figure of £21,850 I shall be driven to cut back on my smoking, switch from gin to elderberry wine, cancel my subscription to *Playmate*, resign from my club and send my wife out to work.

Would emigration work for me? Practically every country is ruled out of consideration by some major handicap. Of the major cricketing nations South Africa is objectionable on account of apartheid, India because it now has the bomb, Pakistan because it is geographically contiguous with India, and Australia and New Zealand because of their Pom-bashing. The Iron Curtain countries are out because their standard-of-living is unattractive, the United States because doctors won't make home calls, Sweden and Denmark because I'm too old for their brand of permissiveness, Greece because of the Colonels, South America because of the lingo . . .

France or Germany would seem to be my best bet. After all, I know them pretty well and have a smattering of their *parlez-vous*. I prefer French bread to ours, I could *live* on German layer-cakes, and though neither country plays cricket the Germans are great at soccer and the French at rugger.

So it could be either country.

Fortunately, there is every sign that inflation in Britain will be no worse than that in Western Europe over the next few years. I mean, it's not much use taking a job in Frankfurt at 36,000 D-marks per annum in the knowledge that to maintain my intake of layer-cake, etc, I'd have to push my income up to 144,000 D-marks by 1978.

It's not, is it?

FINANCIAL ESPIONAGE ON THE 9.20 FROM WOKING

AFTER the Watergate affair most people seem blasé about bugging. They've read their Ian Fleming and they've heard of industrial espionage and they assume that spying is confined to politics and big business. It's my self-appointed task to warn people that bugging is now widely practised against ordinary decent and indecent citizens.

I am not referring to those shady outfits – there appear to be dozens in London and at least one in every village – that pry into our financial affairs and sell information about credit-worthiness to money-lenders, hire purchase dealers, bookies and so on. No, I am concerned with spies who muscle in on our private lives, our plans and intentions and make capital out of information dishonestly acquired and to which, of course, they have no right.

My interest in financial espionage was first aroused on the 9.20 a.m. commuter train from Woking to Waterloo, a train that carries a large number of people who work in the square mile of the City. I am not a City man myself, but I invariably travel by this train because I like to rub shoulders with the men who operate our financial institutions.

They seem to me to be a superior breed and I enjoy their company. They would be amazed, these well-groomed, neatly-dressed gentlemen, to learn that the middle-aged chap in the shabby raincoat who smokes an evil-smelling briar behind a crossword puzzle invariably *remains in the train at Waterloo and returns with it to Woking*.

Some people would consider my behaviour odd, even suspicious, but I can assure you that the idiosyncrasy is completely innocent. Millions watch television nightly, thousands attend football matches: I happen to take pleasure in a daily journey to London and back on the 9.20 from Woking.

What pleasure? Well, if I have to spell it out I suppose it boils down to the fact that City people intrigue me. They smoke better brands of tobacco than I can afford, and speak with an accent redolent of public schools, clubland and the Guards. And I like to think that a little of their polish and social cachet rubs off on to me. Call me a snob if you like. Perhaps I am. I see nothing wrong with a man trying to better himself, especially when he has been forced to spend most of his life in the degrading, poverty-stricken business of journalism.

I will admit that much as I enjoy the tobacco smoke and exquisite accents, it is the burden of my travelling companions' conversation that wows me. They are so well-informed about so many subjects. The weather, for example. They always start on that and are always correct. If one of them ventures 'I thought of popping in at Lord's after lunch – it's going to be a scorcher,' you can be absolutely certain the afternoon will be fair.

They're hot on golf, too, and their stroke-by-stroke accounts of a round at Bramley or Wentworth is thrilling stuff – better than anything you get on TV.

Then there is their 'shop,' by which I mean their discussion of the current financial scene. Fascinating, and so uninhibited. They are so used to my presence that they take me for granted and treat me as part of the upholstery. And I prefer it that way because they are at their best when speaking freely, without reserve of any kind.

Of course, I do not understand much of their highly technical and intelligent discourse, but I listen enthralled as I would to the music of Berlioz or Brahms and take delight in its melody rather than its meaning. Yet there are times when I do understand what they are on about, and these are moments of enormous satisfaction. Once a week, perhaps, one of them will mention some important transaction, some deal in the offing – the re-shuffling of an institutional portfolio, a new merger or takeover or a surprising interim dividend. And for a second or two I have qualms about my conscience.

A man with fewer scruples than I would make instant use of such valuable information, alight at Waterloo and rush to the telephone kiosks. I am simply not made that way. I prefer to sit tight with notebook, pencil, slide-rule and log tables while the train is being swept and serviced at the terminus and to delay my phoning until I am back at Woking. Besides, my friend (a disbarred broker) in Copenhagen Crescent doesn't care to do business much before 11.30.

I suppose I've been lucky. Over the years I've made quite a comfortable living out of deals inspired by conversation overheard on the 9.20. A decent livelihood earned quite fortuitously as a by-product, you might say, of an idiosyncratic leisure activity. Indeed, I sometimes think it would pay unprincipled rogues to gather inside info intentionally by the same route that I choose for purely recreational purposes. And, d'you know, it wouldn't surprise me to learn that some do.

But I am straying from my subject. I set out to discuss FE or Financial Espionage, and I had got as far as the strange happening of the 9.20 to Waterloo. Let me resume.

One morning I had to rush to catch my train. I had breakfasted hurriedly and there had been no time to brush my teeth, and as I lit my pipe behind my crossword I became aware of a foreign body lodged firmly between a couple of molars. I explored with my tongue and discovered that the intruder was a piece of bacon rind.

An embarrassing predicament in such high-toned company!

Five minutes later I had worked the thing lose. Pulling the crossword closer I grabbed the rind between thumb and forefinger and slowly lowered my hand. Then, when I was quite sure that the movement would be unobserved, I worked my fingers beneath the seat and transferred the rind to its underside. But as I did so my fingers encountered an unexpected projection – a small, disc-shaped object. And from it ran a wire.

A hidden microphone. The compartment was bugged! I traced the wire by touch to a tiny hole in the partition or compartment wall, and I knew that some scoundrel, some criminal in the next section of the carriage, was *stealing* information . . . Would you believe it!

Unfortunately, I have left myself no space in which to describe my other discoveries and to expound on FE as planned. But perhaps I have said enough.

WORKERS WANT PAY DECREASE- OFFICIAL

MY friend, Roger K, has a problem. Not the little local difficulty suffered by the eligible young bachelor in the TV commercial, but a problem that haunts him year in year out and for which there is no apparent solution, I can describe this problem most easily by quoting – with his permission – part of the correspondence in which he, his employers and the Treasury have been engaged in recent years.

'The Manager, Alphamo Publishing Corporation. Dear Sir, – You will be aware that I contribute to your magazine under a number of pen-names and earn in an average year the satisfactory sum of £20,000.

'Unfortunately, my earnings are those of a free-lance contributor and are not therefore subject to PAYE; so I pay tax, income and surtax, in lump sums according to annual assessments. I am single and without dependent relatives, my expenses (pen-nibs, ink and paper) are trivial, and consequently the amounts demanded by the collectors total something like £10,000 p.a.

'Though I have little or no difficulty in meeting this tax liability I find the whole exercise distasteful and worrying. I am conscious, even as I write my science fiction yarns under the pseudonyms "Maurice Clover," "Denman Trubshaw," Veronique Delala" and "Hugo Fayne" that I am *incurring* heavy taxes and that a considerable number of people in the offices of Alphamo and the various taxation departments are busying themselves unnecessarily with my affairs. In other words, Sir, I am aware that the accountancy involved in reducing my spendable income from £20,000 to £10,000 is wasteful. Insane even.

'In the circumstances I wonder whether it would be possible for you to reduce my pay to £10,000 (though I would accept £9,000) and make this tax-free? Yours sincerely, Roger K. (alias "Maurice Clover" etc.).'

'Dear K., – Your letter, undated, to hand.

'While I sympathise with you I'm afraid your request is an impossible one. If we were to pay you £10,000 as suggested you would still be required to make the usual returns and to meet demands for income tax and surtax, and these would, I estimate, reduce your net income to something like £6,000.

'We could of course put you on our staff, pay you a salary subjected to PAYE and ease your clerical burden. Would you be prepared to accept £12,000 gross? If not, your best bet would be to put your case to the Chancellor of the Exchequer at 11, Downing Street.

'Please do not hesitate to consult me further if you think I can be of help. Yours faithfully, Cedric Smith, Manager, Alphamo Publishing Corporation.'

Roger K took the manager's advice, wrote to the Chancellor and received the following reply:

'Dear Sir – In the Chancellor's absence I acknowledge your communication of the 15th ultimo. I will see that its content is brought to his notice on his return from various Group of Ten and Committee of Twenty conferences or after his next mini-Budget – whichever is the more remote. Your obedient servant, James Golightly, temporary assistant to the Permanent Secretary of the Parliamentary Secretary to the Treasury.'

Followed by:

'Dear Sir – Further to my communication of September, 1969, I am able to offer the following comment on your somewhat unusual request.

'In Britain it has long been customary to allow Her Majesty's subjects, with a few exceptions, to bargain freely for their wages, salaries, fees and emoluments, with the result that gross pay varies enormously from individual to individual. At present it is possible for the well-to-do to earn as much as 50 times the average wage of the country, though the number of people in this affluent bracket is quite small.

'The conventional wisdom of economic theory maintains that, other things being equal, pecuniary gain is the mainspring of industrial and commercial effort and application.

'We feel, therefore, that your personal contribution to the gross national product would suffer if your earnings were reduced in the way outlined in your letter, and permission to negotiate with the Alphamo Publishing Corporation is therefore refused. Your obedient servant, Timothy Brandynap, secretary to James Golightly. (Dictated and signed in his absence by Martha Snell (Mrs), personal secretary to Mr Brandynap.)'

'Dear Mrs Snell, What about the disincentive effect of taxes that reduce my income from £20,000 to £10,000? Yours, Roger K (written in longhand by the taxpayer and signed in his presence.)'

'Dear Sir, – Your letter to Mrs Snell to hand. You do not seem to realise that high level of taxation is necessary – not, as most people think, to raise funds to finance Government operations, (the printing press can do that), but *to avoid revolution*. If the affluent were allowed to retain their gross incomes and to spend them conspicuously on servants, mansions, luxury yachts and so on, all hell would break loose and the unions would get completely out of hand.

'Though they detest the system the rich would much rather earn high heavily-taxed incomes than lower tax-free incomes, for their nominal (or paper) differentials are precious to them and contribute in no small measure to their *amour propre*.

Hollowood

'You ask me to support my allegations. Very well, I ask you – would a company with vision hire a hall this size year after year for its AGM?'

'Thus a man paying surtax at 75 p.c. is allowed to enjoy the feeling (a) that he is being victimised and robbed by the state, (b) that his taxes are paying the wages of the police and armed services, educating the children of the poor, supporting old age pensioners, building Concordes and providing employment and (c) that some day, possibly, the country will experience a change of heart and permit him to retain a much larger fraction of his gross earnings, his true deserts.

'The fact that these opinions and hopes are ludicrous is neither here nor there, but false or not, they constitute incentives of a sort.

'I trust that my explanation will satisfy you and that we may now consider this correspondence terminated. Your obedient servant, Timothy Brandynap pp James Golightly, Ministry of Posts and Telecommunications, formerly Temp. Asst. to the Perm. Sec., Parl. Sec., Treas.'

PS. Roger K has now retired as a freelance writer and is reading economics on a tax-free grant at Brunel University.

YOU, TOO, COULD DEAL IN CURRENCY

I HOLD currency dealers in awe. Business tycoons, making their living by buying and selling companies, are puzzling enough to a man who considers himself a reckless financier when he entrusts £100 to a building society or a unit trust, but the creatures who earn their keep by trading in currencies are baffling to the point of utter bewilderment.

'What d'you want to be when you grow up?'

'A currency dealer.'

'Really. Are you sure?'

'Absolutely. I can't see myself doing anything else.'

Seems impossible, doesn't it? Yet there must be boys(and girls) who even now are planning to go into business by the year 1990 as dealers in currency. I hope it keeps fine for them.

Whenever I read about people buying yen or selling dollars or cornering marks, I get this feeling that I am being ostracised, cold-shouldered, and that I am missing out on splendid opportunities to support my wife in a manner to which she is unaccustomed. Why, I think to myself, should the pickings of the international money market be reserved for the privileged few? Why shouldn't I dabble?

And I toy with the idea of ringing my bank manager . . .

'Er . . . hello . . . er . . . it's Hollowood here. Is that Mr Flunk?'

'Speaking.'

'Well, er . . . I was wondering whether you'd advise me. I'm thinking of buying marks.'

'Ah, you want our Mr Trifford. He handles travellers' cheques. I'll put you through . . .'

'No, wait. I don't want travellers' cheques. I want marks – D'marks, German mon . . .'

'That's all right, Mr Hollowood. We can let you have notes, but if you're going to be in Germany for more than a day or two I strongly recommend . . .'

'I'm not going to Germany myself.'

'Sorry, sir. One of your family?'

'Nobody's going to Germany.'

'But you said you wanted marks?'

'Well, yes, but as a currency er . . . de . . . er . . . er . . . dealer.'

'A what?'

'A currency dealer. I've been reading in the papers that the mark is undervalued and is likely to appreciate. You must have seen the headlines . . . I say, are you still there, Mr Flunk?'

'Sorry, I was thinking. That *is* Mr Hollowood, isn't it?'

'Of course it is. Joint account No.62 stroke 522418 stroke B.'

'And you want to speculate in marks?'

'Well, not exactly speculate.'

'How many marks have you in mind?'

'Oh, well, that's what I wanted your advice about. Would 200 be reasonable, d'you think?'

'200, eh . . .'

And that's about as far as my toying ever gets.

During the dollar crisis I got very cross with the BBC. They kept on saying that so many millions of dollars had been 'changed' or 'converted' into marks, and I'm quite sure that most listeners got a mental picture of dollar bills being transformed magically into marks. Misleading, of course. Dollars can't be 'changed' into marks: they can only be *exchanged* for marks and it's equally misleading to say, as the papers did that 'buyers of dollars were outnumbered by sellers' or that 'the traffic in pounds was one-way.'

If dollars are sold they are also bought. Every transaction in dollars involves both a seller and a buyer and these twain are brought into existence simultaneously in the same way that the marriage service creates both husband and wife. So on any one day or in any one year the number of dollars sold is precisely equal to the number bought. Precisely! And the traffic is always two-way.

That much, at least, I know.

'Couldn't we just call it The Rate, sir? Base sounds so mean and underhand.'

To the layman the supreme attraction of currency dealing lies in its clinical avoidance of physical contact with money. When you and I think of currency we see stacks of bank-notes, corsetted by elastic bands, with their edges curling like the sandwiches of British Rail. (No, that is unfair. Let's make it British *Railways* or go further back in time to the sandwiches of the LMS.) Stacks of pound notes, dollar bills, lire, francs, drachmas, escudos, pesetas, kroner, guilders, D'marks and yen – notes in every state of preservation from mint-fresh to tatty.

I'll say this for the pound: it's usually in better shape than certain other currency units I could mention. But when we British don't use banknotes to clean our shoes, to mop up soup, coffee or beer, to line hatbands or to serve as spills, blotters, bookmarks and note pads.

No, your currency dealer has no contact with filthy lucre. He picks up the phone and sells so many million dollars, puts the phone down, picks up the phone again and buys the dollars he's sold for marginally less, grins, put on his bowler and tilts it rakishly, hails a cab and hurries into the bar of his club. He's finished for the day – unless he decides to make another cool thou after lunch.

That's the life. It's better than stocks and shares or journalism.

WE HAVE A WEALTH TAX ALREADY

'SAVING is a mug's game,' wrote one financial pundit the other day. 'With money losing its value at a rate of 15 to 20 p.c. per annum savers are chucking the stuff away!'

True or false? Mr Denis Healey, Chancellor of the Exchequer would, I think, approve of the statement: he has admitted that he is a confirmed spender, though he has been wise enough to devote a substantial part of his expenditure to the acquisition of bricks and mortar.

But Mr Aitken L. Parish, who downs a vodka and lime with me from time to time in the Grapes, considers the statement tommyrot.

'Economists tell us,' he said, 'that people tend to save more when rates of interest are high and less when rates are low. My experience is exactly the opposite. During all those years when Bank Rate was a mere 2 p.c. I saved like mad: I *had* to in order to accumulate. Then when BR and interest rates generally shot up I found I could achieve the same return on my money by saving less. I should have thought that was obvious.'

'We were talking about inflation,' I reminded him.

'I was coming to that,' he said. 'Inflation is a wealth tax for most middle class people. It eats into one's capital and under present conditions it converts a nominal interest rate of 12 or 14 p.c. into a negative interest rate. So if I've decided to hoard £x of purchasing power for my retirement I'm compelled to save at an ever-increasing rate. Obvious, isn't it?'

'Don't you envy spenders though?' I said.

'The property dealers and speculators, perhaps, but not those people who spend on consumer goods, lash out on food, clothes, cars, and holidays. On riotous living. The more they spend, the less they save and the higher the rate of interest that borrowers have to pay *me*. When I'm the only saver left I shall be able to exact a really stiff rate of interest – 50 or 60 p.c., say, or 500 or 600 p.c. – and when that happens I may get ahead of inflation.'

'How do your savings now compare with what they were ten years ago?' I said.

'Oh, they're down,' he said, 'in terms of purchasing power. In 1964 I could have bought three decent houses with my capital: now, I'd be lucky to afford one detached villa in Hampstead. But that doesn't worry me unduly.'

'Really?' I said. 'In spite of saving hard for ten years you've thrown away a lot of capital, and you don't mind?'

'No. You see, I'm still *relatively* well off. People who stopped saving when inflation got into top gear are now more or less broke. They've nothing to fall back on – well, nothing but memories of luxury holidays, wardrobes full of out-of-date clobber and a few *objects d'art* that were bought as investments and turn out to be junk – whereas I still have enough capital to live on for ten years even under conditions of galloping inflation.'

Like Mr Parish I am a saver, though I think my aims are on a somewhat loftier plane. I have little hope of hoarding enough cash to see me comfortably through my declining years, so I devote much of my time to propaganda in support of higher pensions. Old age pensions.

Pensions are paid, of course, out of current production, the stuff (food, clothing, baccy, newspapers, etc) being churned out by people still at work, and to get them increased we have to persuade the relatively young to accept a slimmer slice of the gross national product and leave a fatter slice for senior citizens. So I write about a dozen letters a week to influential youngsters like the presidents of the Oxford and Cambridge Unions, the chairmen of the Young Conservatives and the secretaries of the Junior Carlton, the Festival of Youth, the Fabian Cadets and the Young Persons' TUC, urging them to throw their weight behind the Posh Pensions Movement. We want £100 a week for a single pensioner, £180 for a married couple, with a threshold agreement linking the size of the grant to the price of a tot of whisky.

It's my only hope.

Why do I save? Well, without wishing to sound holier-than-thou or excessively disinterested, I do so because I prefer to *give* rather than have my money stolen. By investing in building societies, for example, I know that I am handing my money to the Government and to borrowers, and in my mind's eye I see a handsome young couple gratefully paying off part of the interest on their mortgage with my hard-earned lolly.

I also buy shares, and over the years I've acquired the knack of investing only in companies that produce abysmal results year after year. The dividends I receive, after tax, are minuscule and are promptly reinvested, but I derive pleasure from the thought that some investor has rid himself of a millstone while some stockbroker's wife will benefit from the smile I have limned on her husband's features. Occasionally, I buy unit trusts and bonds and as their value dwindles I am uplifted by a mental image of the happy man who did not purchase my particular mess of pottage.

I've tried spending my money and I don't like it. I'm too old to adjust to a price level that is sheer daylight robbery and definitely unlevel. My dependent son can fork out £10 for a moderate meal for two with equanimity. I can't: I remember four of us consuming excellent steak and chips in a private room at the Grand Hotel, Coketown, for fifteen shillings all told! From time to time I see something I'd like in a shop window, but the price sickens me and I turn away. As I've said, I'd rather give my money away.

The other day I made an inventory of my possessions – books, shoes, pullovers, pyjamas, watch, ballpoints – and decided that they need not be renewed for some time. I shall not become an active customer again until I am a pensioner. By then I shall be able to purchase again with a clear conscience and with money I have not exactly earned. £180 per week is the target and I can hardly wait.

THEORIES OF RELATIVITY

IT NOW seems certain that the major social and economic problems of the Seventies will be concerned with pay relativities. Traditionally wages and salaries have been determined roughly by the interplay of supply and demand, but many people now believe that pay should reflect the pleasantness or unpleasantness of each job. So it will not surprise you to learn that workers who are relatively affluent are already preparing the defensive evidence they hope to give before some new and authoritative Relativities Board.

In the Horse and Compasses the other day a property dealer tried to justify an income (after tax) roughly five times that of the coal-face miner. He began by saying that he'd actually been down a mine for a look-see and had found it 'warm and cosy.' 'Miners are lucky,' he said, 'in that there's no smoking in the pits. This not only saves them a lot of money but frees them from some of the diseases to which property dealers are subject. Then, again, the miner's work involves the use of all his muscles so that he develops a fine physique quite naturally as a by-product of his labours.

'You will see very few miners,' he went on, 'who wear spectacles. This is because they do not have to strain their eyes, as property dealers do, examining the small print of contracts and agreements.

'I have heard miners complaining about the dirt and coal dust that settles on their sandwiches, and in the same breath complaining about the poor light in the mines! Well, they can't have it both ways, can they? The light can't be all that bad if they can detect thumb-prints on a jam butty. In any case, it's a medical fact that the human body operates most efficiently when the food intake includes a certain amount of roughage, and I can think of no roughage more acceptable than specks of dirt and coal that have been lying a mile deep for millions of years, completely uncontaminated by the filth and pollution of man's environment on the earth's surface.'

'By paying £25 a month for 13 years for a deferred term annuity you could stop worrying about my school fees and save yourself, according to my calculations, about £1,000.'

The property dealer's argument is ingenious and impressive.

And typical. A company director told me that he was worth every penny of his £15,000 fee. 'The miner's job may be dirty and dangerous,' he said, 'but at least it is *respected*. For months now pundits of all parties have been saying that the miner is the salt of the earth and a key figure in the country's survival. But you can't open a paper without seeing some disparaging reference to company directors. Our name is *mud*, and it's only fair that we should be recompensed in some financial manner. You never see the headline "miner on sex charge," but the popular Sunday papers keep lines of type reading "Company Director Bound Over" permanently set up.

'Then there's the risk of marital troubles. Company directors are surrounded by attractive secretaries and chicks from the typing pool, and however we react we're always under suspicion. Take me, for example. I've been divorced three times, yet I've never laid a finger on any of the office females. How I envy the miner his cloistered, masculine workplace!'

'Yes, I'm paid considerably more than a miner and I deserve to be,' a bank manager told me. 'Banking may not be as taxing physically as hewing coal, but it can be hazardous. We can trust nobody. Sweet old ladies can pull a gun on us at any moment and hiss "Stick 'em up!" and we can never know for certain whether our strong room is being tunnelled into by gangs of robbers. And as for dirt I definitely prefer the collier's *clean* dirt to the stuff we have to handle. People think it's glamorous to handle stacks of money, but if they knew where banknotes had been and who's handled them they'd realise that the term "filthy lucre" is no exaggeration. Lick your index finger instead of using the sponge pad while you're counting notes and you find yourself in an intensive care unit!'

Finally, I discussed relativity with a footballer who gets £150 a week basic plus a bonus payment of £15 for a win. 'Considerin' we 'ave to 'ang up our boots at about 30 I don't fink we're overpaid' he said. 'A miner can carry on till 'e drops, can't he? And 'e 'as a nice fringe benefit o' free coal. I didn't realise 'ow valuable fringe benefits could be until a monf or so ago when I started collectin' the toilet rolls chucked at us from the kop. My missis was pleased as Punch with 'em 'cos she 'asn't been able to get 'em in the shops. Mind you, she's never satisfied. After the game against Burnley I took her half a dozen and she said "Why can't you pick the daffodil ones, the ones I like instead o' all these borin' whites?" '

It's amazing how much sympathy there is for the miner when we consider how much we lavish on ourselves. It's a mystery that there's enough to go round.

WAGES ACCORDING TO AGE?

IT IS becoming obvious that our present methods of dividing up the national cake are unsatisfactory. Collective bargaining favours the big, tough unions; bargaining at plant level is no use to the employees of companies on the rocks; golden handshakes, tax havens and fringe benefits tend to give capitalism an unacceptable face.

We need a new incomes structure, and no one has a glimmer of an idea what it should be.

In desperation, then, let us look at some of the crackpot notions advanced by the economists and see whether we can find enough sticks to make a platform from which we could launch a real winner.

According to Prof. Herman Schwein, of the University of South Dakota, money really *is* the root of all evil. 'Pay everyone in goods,' he says, 'and we eliminate all the evils of capitalism. People can't hoard hot dinners.' And he is right. But any fool can eliminate the evils of capitalism by eliminating capitalism itself. So goodbye. Prof. Schwein.

'In order to achieve real equality,' says Dr Jules Aout of Bristol, 'every worker should enjoy the services of a top-rate accountant. The advantages won by directors of companies should be available to the humblest employee. There would be less unrest among car workers if they were paid their wages in some tax haven such as the New Hebrides or the Cayman Islands, and if they were allowed free use of company houses and treated to expense account lunches three or four times a week.'

Dr Aout agrees that the training of a new force of some two million tax accountants would cause problems; but 'we can afford it,' he says. 'In fact, the time is rapidly approaching when automation and computerisation will put nearly all manual and semi-skilled workers out of business, and it will be a case of tax accountancy to the rescue.'

What worries me about Aout's plan is the old problem *quis custodiet ipsos custodes*? Or who will control the tax accountants? These clever little men in their pin-stripes and heavy horn-rimmed spectacles would obviously employ *super* tax accountants to look after their own affairs. I can imagine the outcome: a privileged plutocracy accustomed to platinum handshakes, tax havens conveniently situated at the bottom of the garden and fringe benefits the size of drop curtains. So I reckon Aout is out.

'It's what I feared – the synthetic beef extrusion plant now wants us to devise a substitute for soya beans.'

What next? How about Cyril Duluth's scheme to pay everyone according to age? At 21 you get £21 a week, at 50 you get £50 a week, and so on. Well, I like the simplicity of the system and I think it would engender a certain respect for senior citizens. Grandpa, aged 95, would no longer be a nuisance to be off-loaded into some institution: his £95 per week would prove a handy addition to the family income and he'd be cosseted and cocooned and kept alive as long as possible.

As a man already approaching senior citizenship I rather fancy the idea of becoming a sugar-daddy to a team of chicks earning, say, £18 or £19 a week.

Then how about Prof. Selwyn Knuck, of the London School of Economics, who believes that life in the neotechnic State will inevitably become more and more boring for more and more workers unless income distribution is geared to the ubiquitous British love of gambling. Prof. Knuck wants everyone's weekly wage pulled out of a giant hat, a bigger and better 'Ernie.'

Every Friday morning the post would bring us a chit from the Minister of Incomes:

'I am sorry/happy/delighted, to inform you that your net pay this week will be £20/£40/£100.

'The cashier at your place of employment or unemployment will honour this document on presentation.'

The professor is convinced that this system would appeal to our sporting instinct, improve morale and spark off a substantial improvement in productivity.

Unfortunately, the scheme would satisfy our appetite for gambling and destroy the business of such institutions as the pools, the Tote, Premium Bonds, bookies, bingo halls and casinos; and the Exchequer would lose the £175 millions it collects annually from gaming and betting taxes.

So Prof. Knuck's wages gamble would produce appalling unemployment and deal a crushing blow at our natioonal finances. For these reasons it must be considered a non-starter. A pity, but the professor clearly has not done his homework.

IS PROFIT IMMORAL?

WE LIVE in permissive, licentious times. Almost anything goes. The *Guardian*, sometimes known as 'the nonconformist conscience' of Britain, gets away with four-letter words galore, TV is allowed to screen 'Andy Warhol' and publishers can sell their *Nasty Tales*. Lord Longford, Mary Whitehouse and the Apostles of Light struggle against a sea of porn and have difficulty in persuading the public that the vilest smut is *de trop*.

In fact, only one word in the English language is labelled dirty with any consistency – profit.

Why should this be? The word has an impeccable ancestry and is satisfying to both eye and ear, yet it has been saddled with noxious overtones, and even dyed-in-the-wool capitalists shrink from using it blatantly. There are, indeed, times when in the interests of diplomacy they replace it with such euphemisms as margin, gain, balance, earnings, recompense and remuneration.

In an attempt to solve the mystery I conducted a probe into people's attitudes to profit . . .

James Preamble, car-fitter, of Coventry told me: 'It's obvious man! You've heard of the Excess Profits Tax, haven't you? Well, that's a complete give-away. If profits were above-board there'd be no need to describe any part of them as excess. You've never heard of excess wages or salaries, have you? 'Course not.

'What d'you call a bloke who makes profits? A profiteer, or a filthy profiteer. Know what I am? A wage-*earner*, not a *wageer*! Profit is ill-gotten gain, money for jam, a swindle. The bosses define it as the difference between income and expenditure, between buying-price and selling-price. But why should there be *any* difference? Why can't everything be non-profit-making?'

'Just a minute,' I said. 'Tell me, what d'you get as a fitter?'

'£45, and I earn every penny of it.'

'And you think you deserve a profit of £25 a week on the wage of the average nurse?'

'Profit! What profit? The difference in pay is called a differential, you ignorant basket! Differential!'

'All right,' I said, 'let's look at it another way. You sell your labour . . .'

'Skill!'

'Sorry, you *sell* your skill for £45 a week – right? How much does it *cost* you to live, bring up your family? In other words, how much d'you manage to save?'

'Precious little. A fiver at the most.'

'Well, that's your profit, the difference between cost and selling price. It works out at 12½ per cent. You're working for a profit of 12½ per cent.'

Mr Preamble was speechless, but he managed to blow his whistle and a mate at the next bench yelled, 'Everybody out!'

My next customer was a Mrs Marlene Tissue of Coventry. 'Profit?' she said. 'D'you mean the stuff they stick on at the shops? It's disgusting. I bought a plastic mixing-bowl the other day for 60p and when I got it home and removed the label there was a smaller label underneath marked 40p and, believe it or not, there was a third label under that saying 2s 6d. That's profit for you! They're all the same shopkeepers! All on the make!'

'Surely,' I said, 'the example you've given me is exceptional?'

'No, the butcher weighs his thumb with the meat, the grocer says "3p off," but only after he's stuck 8p on, the baker charges an extra 1p for a bun with a currant, the plumber charges for forgetting his tools, the publican pulls you a stout into a glass containing half an inch of water, the electrician . . .'

'All right,' I said, 'I take your point. It must be very difficult these days for housewives.'

'I'll say! Especially when they do two jobs, like me.'

'Oh, you go out to work then?'

'Not really. I help Jack when he's busy. We have a greengrocery business.'

The Rev. Arthur Psalter of St Morbid's, Morpath, said: 'Yes, there are harsh words about profit and usury in the good book and it does seem that most of the regulars among my flock are business men looking for forgiveness. Still, I value their advice, their know-how. It was Sir Harold's idea to start the collection plates with 50p pieces and so make it thoroughly embarrassing for the congregation to give less. We've upped our takings by 180 per cent. since Sir Harold joined the church council. And I'm immensely grateful to Mr Maudsley, another parishioner, who lectures in psychology at the university. He put a stop to "pew shrinkage" – our name for petty theft – by stamping all our Prayer Books and Bibles with the words "To Be Taken Away" instead of "Not To Be Taken Away." Amazing, really.

'For years we'd had no bellringers at St Morbid's, and no one to pump the organ either. But we're going great guns since Sir Harold started his Ecclesiastical Slimming Group. They queue up nowadays to try their hands at campanology, etc. And I don't suppose there are many parishes that make their own communion wine *and* sell it – under a different label, of course – to the bingo club. That was Mr Camp's idea.'

I spoke next with Max Weltan of Lloyd's. 'I blame the Government,' he said. 'They're always apologising for profits and telling the country they're going to freeze or squeeze them. But the biggest profiteer in Britain is the Government itself. It prints money for practically nothing and flogs it to the banks at 100p to the £, and I make that a profit of almost 100 per cent.

'Then look at its pensions schemes. Males contribute throughout their lives to national insurance which is supposed to guarantee them a pension at 65. But life expectancy among males is only 69 which means that the average worker draws his pension for only four years! Millions of men paying national insurance will snuff it *before* the age of 65, so their return on their contributions is nil. How's that for profiteering?'

'But surely,' I said, 'isn't that the way you underwriters make your money – by insuring ships that never sink, fires that never break out, parents who never breed triplets, lightning that never strikes and village fetes that are never cancelled because of inclement weather? If that's not profit I don't know what is.'

'You're forgetting,' he said, 'that unlike MPs, we have un-limited liability. We have to be worth at least £100,000 and if things go badly we can lose the shirts off our backs. And we don't make profits, we get returns.'

Finally, I quizzed Lord Thomkins of Grub Street, the news-paper magnate and TV tycoon who once declared that a fran-chise in commercial telly was 'a licence to print your own bread.'

'That is a statement I regret having made,' he said. 'It is true that profits were high in the early days, and it is true that we still have our licence. What I didn't figure on was the way printing costs – banknote paper and the metal thread that runs through it, inks, presses, labour and so on – would rocket. Why, I guess it would be cheaper nowadays to print counterfeit money, and that's a fact.'

PART 3
OFFICE MATTERS
MOSTLY

WHEN THE CASH-FLOW SLOWS TO A TRICKLE

IN A TIME of crisis it is no disgrace to clutch at straws. Is there, perhaps, a lesson to be learned from the behaviour of Burnley Football Club which manages to keep its head above water financially only by selling a star player every other year?

The club, chaired appropriately enough by a well-known butcher, has recently financed the erection of a new stand by disposing of Martin Dobson to Everton for £300,000. Burnley is too small a town to support First Division soccer in competition with your Liverpools and Manchesters, so it balances the books by flogging its human capital.

Not so very long ago a man could ease himself of impecuniosity by auctioning his wife (there's a graphic account of such a deal in Thomas Hardy's 'The Mayor of Casterbridge') and though open market transactions involving the sale – not the *swapping* – of wives is now illegal it is not unknown for husbands in the red to toy with the idea of offering their partners to the highest bidder.

At first sight then there is little scope in Britain for dealing in flesh and blood. In America decent blood fetches a fair price and a man who can mass produce the stuff without obvious adulteration need never lack the price of a meal. A cup of tea, with sugar, is the most one can expect in Britain for an armful of grade A gore. But harking back to soccer I seem to remember that just after the war, when domestic servants were in desperately short supply for the first time, it was rumoured that Lady De Witt Colfax-Netherly had made an offer of £10,000 for Arsenal's reserve left-back. She was in urgent need of a butler-gardener.

A year or so ago the City was electrified by news that the chairmen of two rival blue chip soap companies (blue chips, by the way, were company shares considered to be almost as safe as the Bank of England) had been seen dining at the Ivy restaurant. These tycoons hated each other's guts and the only inference to be drawn from their meeting was that a take over was in the wind. For three weeks there was great activity among punters and the shares of both companies fluctuated wildly. But there was no statement from the rivals and eventually the market calmed down and proceeded to turn its attention to other scraps of tittle-tattle.

Later, however, it leaked out that there had been a takeover of sort, for some newshound discovered that Merle Smith, formerly private secretary to the first soap magnate was now girl Friday to the second. Merle was and is an absolute gem, and not bad looking either, and it was said at the time that her transfer fee, of which she took a 5 p.c. cut, ran into five figures.

So there is still hope for businessmen suffering from cash-flow difficulties. You may be short on stock and equipment and you may have exhausted every hope of further help from the banks: and in consequence you may be thinking about cutting the costs by reducing your staff. But before committing yourself take a good look at your human assets.

Miss Cheavers, say, who's such a dab hand with the copying machine – have you really assessed her value correctly? She's been with you for nearly two years and you've hardly noticed her. True, you've glanced conjecturally in her direction once or twice, but you've been put off rather by her nose and her chewing-gum. But you know damn well that she'd be difficult to replace. She's highly efficient, cooperative, quiet (except for the gum) and loyal. And you know too that Bill Tandem, boss of AIK, is always yapping at the club about his inability to find good secretarial material and about his distaste for gold-digging temps.

It could well be that Miss Cheavers would suit Bill down to the ground, and his company is loaded.

'What d'you suppose would happen to the country if brokers went on strike, like you car workers, just because they were dissatisfied with pay and conditions?'

Miss Crabstanley? The gorgeous Janice Crabstanley? No, perish the thought! The girl's a jewel and you'd as soon lose your right eye. There aren't many p.a. secretaries who can take shorthand at speed, type neatly, spell accurately, make drinka-ble coffee *and* look absolutely stunning. But yours is a small business languishing for want of cash, and there must be a market, a really significant market, for Jan, or rather Miss Crabstanley. You won't let her go, of course, but it would do no harm to mention her talents and her availability at the next meeting of Rotarians.

Naturally, you wouldn't make your intentions too obvious. There's no law against *private deals* involving the transfer of female secretaries, but I've an idea that the unions and Mr Heath would very properly say something about the unacceptable face of capitalism if the deals became public knowledge. In 1971 when the *Financial Times* index was up in cloud-cuckooland and rising there was something of a scandal when a certain Jasper McFee was accused of cornering the market in attractive City secretaries. McFee ran a 'bucket shop' import-export business, dealing ostensibly in caraway seed and linoleum from a warehouse off Fenchurch Street, and this, to knowing City types, was familiarly known as 'The Windmill' because it housed an extraordinary number of nubile and highly qualified Girl Fridays.

Rumour had it that the girls, all well paid, were 'sold' as and when brokers, merchant bankers and insurance companies were driven frantic by arrears of typing, docketing and so on, and that large sums of money changed hands with each 'sale.' Another view, however, was that McFee was merely a libidinous millionaire married to a termagant.

The whole sordid business may have been pure fiction because when last heard of McFee was commissionaire at a beri-beri colony in Zaire, and I only mention it to illustrate my thesis that there is still money to be made in the white slave traffic. It embarrasses me to state this openly. In my defence I can only plead hard times. Sorry.

(I was unable to persuade my wife to type this article and I apologise in advance for any errors that may have crept into the text.)

OFFICE ECONOMIES

THE wave of austerity that is sweeping the country is not without its effects on traditional company hospitality. My spies tell me that Rolls-Royces, Daimlers, Mercs and Jags have given way to Cortinas, Datsuns and Dafs, and that more and more Girl Fridays are expected to spend part of their day as uniformed chauffeurs.

It is not generally realised that *regular* boardroom lunches are regarded by the commissioners as taxable perquisites and that expense account meals are deductible only when the guests include *bona fide* foreign business representatives. So there has been a marked change in the eating and drinking habits of top executives, as I discovered the other day when I was invited to the offices of Omniflex Holdings (1937) Ltd.

The usual drill in the chairman's sanctum at Omniflex is for Lord Straynes to open up the cunningly concealed refrigerator in his Komposit Kabinet and extract ice while muttering the incantation 'Usual?' Then enormous glasses of gin or whisky on the rocks are poured and cigars passed round. I sensed the change of atmosphere as soon as I alighted from the tandem guided by Lord Strayne's ex-chauffeur and was led to the goods lift.

There were two directors with the chairman and one of them was chewing gum vigorously in an attempt to stave off his craving for tobacco. The chairman was playing with one of those swinging balls gimmicks and the other director was nibbling at his finger-nails.

They were as welcoming as ever except that the Komposit Kabinet remained locked. We talked of this and that, but mostly about cash flow problems, until we were all ravenously hungry and the air was filled with the rumbling of stomachs.

Suddenly, the chairman pressed a switch on his intercom and said 'When you're ready, Sandra,' and almost immediately a nubile blonde entered bearing a sliced loaf, a packet of margarine and a tin of corned beef.

'Economy campaign,' said Straynes. 'Hope you don't mind?'

'Not at all,' I said. 'I'm all for it. And I'm particularly fond of Purox.'

Lord Straynes sighed with relief and fell to opening the can while Sandra spread marge.

'You've forgotten the mustard,' said Coles, the younger of the two directors.

'Oh, no we haven't,' said the chairman, placing an index finger along his nose in a gesture suggestive of Machiavellian cunning. And he produced a jar of Colman's ready-mix from a waistcoat pocket.

The sandwiches were washed down with two bottles (between four of us) of a well-known pale ale. The food was dryish but filling and satisfying.

'We've closed down the executive dining rooms and are saving upwards of £5,000 a week,' said Lord Straynes, 'in catering bills. Every little helps, you know.'

'But the men?' I said 'They still have their canteen don't they? Couldn't you eat there?'

'Matter of fact, we tried it,' said Coles, 'but the men wouldn't have it. Claimed they found our presence inhibiting, accused us of snooping and complained about the soup on the only two occasions we joined them. Said it was turtle – which, of course, it wasn't.'

I asked about other economies.

'Well, we no longer have special cigarettes made up for us by Tribourg and Fremlin, and Havanas are almost unknown. We still have morning coffee, but the Sèvres and Limoges went to Sotheby's in June and now it's just paper cups from the vending machine. Ditto with the Spode and afternoon tea.'

'And dining out with foreign buyers?' I said.

'We did a check a year ago and discovered that in the previous year we'd entertained 5,260 Japs – I've got the figures here – 12,216 Frenchmen, 9,201 Germans, 24,003 Americans, 74 Chinese, 3,240 Danes . . . I mean, it was quite ridiculous. We were terrified what would happen if the Inland Revenue became suspicious, so we decided that every foreign buyer should be vetted personally by the chairman and that expenditure per head on entertaining should never exceed £10 per night.'

'And did it work?' I asked.

'Not really,' said Coles. 'If our guests fancied a theatre or a strip club it meant we had to restrict the food to a beef burger at a Lyons, and, of course, fancy drinks like champers were completely out. Now that the museum and art gallery charges are being dropped we're making the Tate and the National Gallery our chief attractions. Trouble is, they close so early. Still, there's always Buck House, Downing Street, Speakers' Corner and Fleet Street.'

'I hope,' I said, 'that your economies won't cut out your pourboires at Christmas. I don't mind admitting that your Harrods hamper has in the past made all the difference to my family's festive season.'

'Gone, definitely gone,' said the chairman. 'We hate doing it, but it was becoming too much of a good thing. Last year we had 3,500-odd recipients on our list and not all of them were grateful. Some old customers actually had the nerve to write in and criticise the contents of the hampers, and some wanted us to organise an exchange and mart for them so that unwanted quails in aspic (say) could be swapped for an extra dish of pâté de foie gras, or a bottle of Crofts' could be offered for two dozen halves of Guinness. Oh, it was becoming impossible. So this year we're sending diaries, pocket diaries with maps of the Underground as end-papers and Continental holidays marked in red. This should save us another £20,000.'

'Well,' I said, 'it's all very sad, but I can see that it's necessary. You're not cutting directors' emoluments, I suppose?'

'No room for manoeuvre there. I'm afraid,' said Lord Straynes. 'In fact our only other economy will be our contributions to political parties.'

'Parties?' I said.

'Well, party, then. They'll get damn all for four years and on their showing at the general election that's what they deserve. Don't you agree?'

I nodded.

THE GENTLE ART OF SKIVING

THREE items caught my attention. The first was Graham Turner's account of the alleged skiving at British Leyland; the second, the sad story of a secretary who had so little work to do that she spent most of the day painting and repainting her toe nails; and the third, an extract from a Young Liberals manifesto proclaiming that no one should be compelled to work.

So some of us do as little work as possible, some are desperately anxious to do more, and others consider that work should be optional.

In my time I've belonged to each of these groups, and I suspect that you have too. Many years ago I was a business executive occupying an ivory tower of an office. My status was such that two female secretaries were considered a necessary prop to my ego and they were installed in an adjoining office equipped with typewriters, filing cabinets, a copying-machine and a cupboard containing everything needed to supply me with liquid sustenance.

It took me a month to settle in, arrange my desk and drawers and instruct the secretaries about my habits, my preferences concerning tea, coffee, pencils and the presentation of correspondence, and by the end of the month I realised that I could get through a day's work easily in about two hours. When I reported this fact to the boss he said, 'Lucky you!' with a smirk that accused me of blatant sycophancy.

During the second month I made repeated attempts to spin the work out over a seven-hour day. I wrote footling memoranda that circulated sluggishly and were obviously unread. I got rid of one of the secretaries to another executive whose outer office resembled a harem, made my own tea, sharpened my own pencils, and spent a lot of time pacing the wall-to-wall carpet, dialling for the Test score and doodling. At the end of the third month I resigned and sacrificed the best salary I had ever earned. The boredom was killing me.

I am unimpressed by the Turner disclosures. Modern factory production has to be designed to keep the assembly line operating at a speed within the capacity of the least able of its human cogs. And though this means that the more able are less 'stretched' than they would, perhaps, like, it does mean a regime of more or less unremitting and tedious toil for all concerned.

But for an assembly line to run satisfactorily it must carry enough 'surplus' workers to make sure that sickness and absenteeism do not bring it to a halt, so there are times when men are involuntarily idle in employment. And I suggest that it's such men who are reported to be spending half their working hours at card games or kipping.

Should we be made to work? Well, if we have interesting jobs, jobs that tax our skills and ingenuity, there's no problem. Most of the so-called middle classes – but by no means all – positively enjoy their hours of gainful employment and are desperately unhappy when unemployed or prematurely retired. But my definition of work is the stuff we'd avoid like the plague if we could afford to do so, and I believe that the vast majority of factory workers regard work as a necessary evil.

To put the record straight I must add that in my time I've done my share of skiving. In fact I'm still something of a skiver. As a journalist I have evolved ingenious methods of avoiding the cerebration that should precede the putting of pen to paper as writer and cartoonist. Examples:

1. At any hour I can fool myself into the belief that radio and

TV are emitting material of quintessential importance to my work so I justify long hours in front of the screen for Test matches, soccer, Pot Black, John Julius Norwich, Morecambe and Wise and all documentaries as 'raw material collecting.' Ditto with the music of Radio 3.

2. Seated at my desk I spend an unconscionable time making sure that my equipment is in order. I use a Parker pen and this is supported by two back-up pens in case of malfunction. I mean, you never know. Nibs can become crossed, the flow of ink can change with monsoon suddenness or the plastic barrel of the pen could develop plastic fatigue and disintegrate with catastrophic effect. So I tend to delay mental exertion until I am satisfied that the desk is level, stocks of paper are to hand and all pens functioning perfectly.

3. I find it impossible to concentrate unless I am alone. Intruders halt my flow of ideas, especially when I am confronted with an intractable sentence, and if I hear a fly buzzing, or think I do, I cannot proceed until the interloper has been located, slain or removed. And all this takes time. The fact that those near and dear to me are unaffected by the thunderous din made by the common housefly has led them to make the cruel suggestion that I suffer from head noises. But they are wrong. My head and hearing are absolutely normal.

What my wife has not yet tumbled to is the fact that she is married to a skiver.

JOB SATISFACTION FOR THE WHITE COLLAR WORKER

YOU KNOW that scene in the Chaplin film classic, *Modern Times*, where Charlie emerges dazed from a shift on the factory assembly-line suffering from the disease known as fitters' jitters? The poor fellow has been wielding his spanners all day and now, having clocked out, he is still under the spell of the machine and continues mindlessly to repeat his manipulative movements at the conveyor. He is a robot that can't be switched off.

Well, industry is beginning to realise that fitters' jitters is a serious malady and efforts are being made to prevent it. Something called 'job satisfaction' is now, or soon will be, the common goal of industrialists, trade unions, psychiatrists and time-and-motion efficiency experts, a decade or two from now the division and sub-division of labour may be as dead as the dodo, and all workers may once again be craftsmen (or a sort), using their brains and skills, and either enjoying their work or finding it much less of a bore.

But if manual workers need job satisfaction, so do clerical workers, and so far the plight of the man in the white collar has been almost completely ignored. It is taken for granted that office workers, the 'nine to five' brigade, have cushy jobs and are under strain only when fighting to get to and from work in desperately overcrowded trains and buses. This is, of course, sheer nonsense.

The average white-collar worker faces a daily round of stupifying tedium and breaks under the stress much more frequently than his blue-collar comrade. I know. At one time I was employed by the Pennyfeather Research Institute, an industrial relations and research consultancy, and my case-book is a veritable chamber of horrors. I dip into it at random:

Arthur Xenophen Crewe was critical path analyst with a potato crisp manufacturer in Barnsely. He had been recruited straight from Oxford by a managing director who liked the ring of the term 'critical path analysis' and thought it would impress fellow Rotarians and denizens of the nineteenth hole at the Esmeralda Golf Club. Arthur was given an office, a secretary and a good salary and told to get on with it.

For a few months he thanked his lucky stars and tried to look busy. He dictated memoranda, loaded his in-tray with Governmental Green Papers and statistical abstracts, filed his nails, taught his secretary how to make Irish coffee and read the sports pages of three newspapers. But these occupations (and counting lucky stars) consumed only an hour or so of his eight-hour day, and he soon became dreadfully bored and miserable.

In desperation he tried to extend his sphere of influence within the company by helping members of the typing pool with their football coupons, redesigning a label for 'Fishflayvor Crisps' and taking over the captaincy of the darts team. He even tried to interest the board of directors in a scheme to introduce an entirely new line of turnip crisps. But the monotony of his chores began to undermine his health: he developed a nervous tic in his left ear so that his spectacles shook and fell on to his desk blotter every 25 minutes.

It was the glasses that drew my attention to him when I, with four other representatives of the Pennyfeather RI, made our annual inspection of the company. It took me two long lunches with him to discover the root of his trouble, and only a single night on the town with him – at Tommy's, the Kensington Adlon and Quelch's Striparama – to work out a remedial programme.

His job, I decided, was too specialised and too repetitive. I told the managing director that Mr Crewe would be happier and more efficient if he were given a staff of critical path analysts to manage, and my recommendation was accepted.

The change was dramatic. Quite suddenly the three new assistants were competing with Crewe for the secretary's favours. He smartened himself up, became passionately interested in the vetting of his staff's expense accounts, and introduced contract bridge. Their games were played with cards, specially designed for critical path analysis offices, in which the pips are replaced by equivalent computer symbols.

Or take the case of N.P.S. Slackersby, dividend ledger clerk with Molson, Pippet and Molson. Slackersby's job was to record changes in the ownership of the company's shares. He was a conscientious worker who had nothing to do because over the years the equity had been concentrated into just two holdings. The Molsons owned 53 p.c. and Pippet 47 p.c. and neither party had the slightest intention of selling.

Hollowood

'If I'm not to be trusted why d'you suppose the motor insurance people have given me a bonus year?'

Twice a year Slackersby made out three dividend warrants, posted them to the banks of Pippet and the Molsons and typed duplicate returns for Inland Revenue. The rest of his time was spent looking through old ledgers and memorising the names and addresses of former shareholders. Once a week he got an office boy to test his memory. The lad would open one of 23 huge ledgers at random and read out a name. 'Barnes, Mr S.K.,' he would say, and without a moment's hesitation Slackersby would recite 'Montcrieff House, Allenby Road, Taunton, Somerset.'

The man was almost round the bend and there seemed little I could do for him. But I arranged for his job to be restructured and within a year he had recovered and seemed reasonably happy. Now he is quite a craftsman. One corner of his office is partitioned off to form a little stationery and book-binding shop. He makes and binds his own ledgers, cuts his own stationery from stacks of paper supplied by IPC, stamps his letter-heading with a John Bull printing outfit (No.7), folds his own envelopes, makes his own glue and so on. On my last tour of inspection I gave him a JS (Job Satisfaction) rating of 73.

Then there was Henry S.Toehold, City Editor of the *Loamshire Chronicle and Star*. It is a well-known fact that City editors never dabble themselves in the shars they discuss in print. The reason is clear: they haven't the money. Toehold was no exception. On a provincial paper the City section consists almost entirely of syndicated material from London, so Toehold was also 'Nimrod' of the sports pages, 'Elektra' of the astrology column and 'Sacheverell' of 'Home Notes.'

A varied life, you would think, with oodles of JS. But no: Toehold despised all his four hats and hated himself for producing so much drivel. I was called in when the editor of the *Chronicle* discovered three bottles of sleeping capsules in his City editor's desk and feared the worst.

'Look, Toehold,' I said, at our first meeting in private, 'things may be bad, but they're never *that* bad.'

'What's all this about?' he asked.

'You're a relatively young man,' I said. 'You've got a lot to live for.'

'I'll say I have,' he said. 'If you can keep a secret I can tell you that I'm on to something really big – a story that should, if I play my cards properly, put me in line for a job in Fleet Street.'

I thought he was stalling.

'You see these?' he said, opening his drawer and extracting the capsules. 'They're on sale in practically every pharmacy in Britain. Recommended price, 75p for 10 capsules. And d'you know what they're made of? I've just had them analysed by the chemistry master at Nelson Road Comprehensive – chalk!'

'By golly!' I said. 'You've got a scoop there all right. Sell it to the *Sun* or *Mirror*, a slashing attack on the Ministry of Health and . . .'

'Ministry of Health my foot!' exclaimed Toehold. 'It's the Environment people I'm going to expose. I've just been down to Sussex and you should see what these rogues are doing to the South Downs. They've got a chalk quarry there as big as Wembley Stadium.'

Toehold didn't get to Fleet Street. He resigned as City Editor to become a director of a growing pharmaceutical company, and now he has plenty of money for speculation.

PAYOLA IN THE CITY

POLITICIANS aren't the only people, you know, who are asked to open fetes, unveil portraits and make founders' day speeches, so they're not the only recipients of mementoes such as shields, ashtrays, coffee pots and fountain pens. In fact, as I look around my study I can see half a dozen objects that would cause me acute embarrassment if I were asked to explain them.

For example, on my desk there's a nickel-plated cup of the trophy type in which I keep my pencils. It is clearly marked 'SS Empress of New Zealand' and was a consolation prize in a shuffleboard competition held – oh, long, long ago. (I have put it like that because the Commissioners of Inland Revenue have such incredible memories.) I can imagine the duologue between the relentless QC and the present owner of the cup . . .

QC: You say it was a consolation prize? Does that mean you were disappointed not to receive a present of greater value?

HOLLOWOOD: Oh, no. It so happened that I was sitting at the purser's table and I told him I'd have won the shuffleboard competition if the ship had been as steady as she was claimed to be. I'm bitterly ashamed about it now: I was being a thoroughly bad sport.

QC: I see. And the purser, knowing you to be a journalist, thought you might write critically about the ship?

HOLLOWOOD: I don't think so. It was all over in a minute. I lost my temper and called the vessel 'a rolling hell-ship' and an hour later when I got back to my cabin there was this cup and a card saying: 'With the Captain's compliments.'

QC: So the cup was intended to buy your silence?

HOLLOWOOD: But that's ridiculous. I never write about shipping. I was the paper's chess correspondent.

QC: How much is the cup worth?

HOLLOWOOD: Nothing. I gave it to the cricket club jumble sale five years in succession, but no one ever wanted it.

QC: Very well, let's turn to this gold table lighter with the inscription 'Gratefully, Prestonbrook.' The signature is that of Lord Prestonbrook, chairman of TEC breweries. What, may I ask, was he grateful for?

'If I'd taken your advice and sold when the index was at 400, we'd now be facing a crippling wealth tax.'

HOLLOWOOD: It was all a mistake. You see, I was sent along to cover the AGM of TEC at the Dorchester and . . .

QC: What was a chess correspondent doing covering an annual general meeting?

HOLLOWOOD: Oh, in those days we were expected to do a bit of everything. Well, when I got there I had a few drinks with the TEC people and discovered I was the only reporter present. So I nipped off and went to the pictures, and afterwards wrote out my report from the chairman's statement which had been circulated beforehand. And the next day I got a phone call from Lord Prestonbrook's secretary saying it was jolly decent of me not to mention the rumpus. Apparently, some of the sharehol-ders at the meeting had kicked up a fuss and demanded the board's resignation. I didn't want to admit that I'd skipped the actual meeting, so I said to the secretary, 'It seemed a storm in a teacup to me and I couldn't see any point in flying off the handle.' And two days later I received the lighter. It's never worked, but I'm told it's worth £25 and I use it as a paper-weight.

QC: Have you ever owned shares in TEC?

HOLLOWOOD: Well, yes. I had a few at the time, but I sold them on the day I received the lighter. I didn't fancy a company that would chuck away the shareholders' money on gold light-ers.

QC: Did you sell at a profit?

HOLLOWOOD: No, I lost heavily. A month later TEC made a takeover bid for Bewdleys, the cigarette lighter people, and the shares climbed from a few shillings to . . . Well, roughly what they are today. Altogether, I suppose, I must have lost . . .

QC: All right, all right, let's move on to this transistor radio. Was that a memento?

HOLLOWOOD: In a way. One week I wrote my chess column under the heading 'White Knight Sweeps The Board' and to my amazement a Japanese company selling transistor radios quoted those very words in its advertisements. The company's latest model was called 'White Knight,' you see. I felt a bit of a fool seeing my words and my name used in this way to recom-mend Jap radios, so I complained to my editor.

QC: And?

HOLLOWOOD: Nothing happened. We were very short of ads at the time. Besides, the Japs sent the editor a free transistor too. It's a good set. I can get Australia direct on it. For the cricket, the Tests, you know.

QC: Finally, we come to a memento that should take quite a bit of explaining. I refer of course to the Epstein bust of H.G. Wells. Another present, Mr Hollowood?

HOLLOWOOD: You're not going to believe this. In the late Fifties an eccentric bachelor, Sir Norris Sidewinder, chairman of the Snacker and Diplocket Small Things (1928) Ltd. and an enthusiastic chess player, invited me to spend the weekend with him at his country retreat, Diplocket Towers. I didn't want to miss the village cricket match against Rexpuddle, but because Snacker and Diplocket were co-sponsor with my paper of the Mercian Chess Championship I felt it impolitic to refuse.

At the time I was a learner-driver and when I rolled up to the Towers in my Sunbeam-Talbot Sir Norris was very angry. He was a JP, you see, and he knew – as I did – that it is illegal for a learner to drive unaccompanied.

'I'm surprised at you, Hollowood,' he said. 'I thought you were a responsible citizen!'

I said I was sorry and that I'd remove the L-plates before making the return journey, and for some reason this made him even more angry.

'You'll do no such thing!' he said. 'Leave it to me. I'll think of something.'

Well, after a pretty drab weekend I thanked him and prepared to take my leave. He strolled with me to my car. To my astonishment the bust was on the passenger seat.

'It's the best I can do,' said Sir Norris. 'I've tried all my other pieces of sculpture, but the H.G. Wells looks the most realistic. And never, *please*, drive unaccompanied again while you're a learner.'

Frankly I thought he was dotty, but I decided to humour him so I said. 'You're most considerate, sir. I'll send the bust back as soon as I get home.'

'You'll do nothing of the sort,' he said. 'I've been trying to get rid of that damned thing for years.'

And that's how it came into my possession. So help me!

QC: I think the court has heard enough. You may stand down.

THE THEORY OF TIPPING

IN COMMON with 99.35 per cent of the people of Britain I loathe tipping. The other .65 per cent either don't mind it or positively enjoy doling out less than the recipient feels he has a right to expect.

My worst experience as a tipper occurred in Los Angeles when I was somewhat inexperienced as a globetrotter and even more hard up than I am today. One autumn evening I had to leave my room on the 18th floor of the Ritz-Sheraton to keep a speaking engagement with the local branch of the Bimetallist Society. The trouble with air-conditioned rooms on 18th floors is that occupants have little idea what the weather is like at street level, so that when I descended to the lobby, coatless, I was surprised to find myself confronted by a rainstorm of monsoon intensity.

I stood watching the cascade for five minutes or so and then glanced at my watch. The convention hall was only fifty yards away, just across the street, but to venture forth even for five seconds would have meant a drenching. Quandary. I was not at the time a frequenter of taxis and my economic mind shuddered at the very idea of paying through the nose for such a minute journey.

I consulted my watch again and then approached a giant clad in a long vermilion coat with brass buttons and a cap loaded with gold braid. The commissionaire put two fingers to his mouth and emitted a whistle so piercing that it would have shattered every pane in the Crystal Palace, and almost immediately a yellow cab swished to a halt in front of the hotel.

All but a yard of the pavement was protected from the deluge by the hotel canopy, and as I grabbed the handle of the taxi door and felt the rain beating a tattoo on my skull, it suddenly struck me that I was committing a social solecism. Commissionaires expect to be rewarded for their musical renditions.

I selected a quarter (of a dollar) from a fist-full of coins and flicked it with my thumb in the direction of the commissionaire. This was neither the time nor the place for niceties of behaviour. I watched the coin spin six yards, strike him on the chest, fall to earth and roll into the gutter. In a fraction of a second he had identified the tip and spurned it as an insult to his uniform and standing.

I blushed, opened the taxi door, dived into the gutter, pocketed the quarter and scrambled to shelter. A thoroughly nasty experience.

We all know that NO TIPS backwards reads SPIT ON. I first became acquainted with this anagram in a small restaurant when a villainous-looking waiter tried to bully me. I had just taken a frugal, lonely lunch in the Cromwell Road, during an interval between exams at the Imperial Institute, when I became aware of the waiter's hovering presence. He stood with legs crossed, leaning against my table with one hand only inches from the saucer bearing the receipted bill and my change, and his mission was obvious from his ominous scowl.

I had not exactly covered myself in glory in the morning's paper in economic history and in consequence my normally sunny disposition was not in operation. But instead of saying 'What the hell are you standing there for, you greasy toad?' I merely pointed to the 'No Tips' sign on the wall.

'Read it backwards!' he said with a leer.

'Spit on,' I said, 'what's that supposed to mean?'

'What it says! The notice is just for decoration. Gratuities are part of our pay.'

'I shall report you to the manager!' I said.

'You'll be lucky!' he said. 'He's at Ascot all this week.'

I became alarmed and glanced round the room in search of support. All the tables were now deserted – except one where a little old lady sat reading a Penguin and toying with spaghetti.

'Excuse me, madam,' I shouted, and the quiver in my voice surprised me, 'do you tip in this place?'

'Certainly not,' she said. 'Can't you read?'

'Read it backwards!' said the waiter.

She was coolness itself. She whipped off her reading glasses and slowly looked the waiter up and down. Then she turned her head and consulted the notice.

I stood and took two paces towards her. I wanted to tell her she mustn't let herself be ordered about by the blackguard, that I was sorry I'd interrupted her meal.

'Tips no' she said. 'That's what it says backwards. Why?'

I exploded with laughter.

'Thank you very much, ma'am,' I said. 'This miserable waiter was trying to pull a fast one. *Demanding* a tip!'

'But why did he want me to read it backwards?' she said.

'No idea,' I said. 'I think he's barmy.'

I looked round anxiously to see whether he'd overheard, but he had retreated.

'Thank goodness for that!' I said. 'Thank you.'

I collected my change and hurried back to the Imperial Institute.

For some reason I found concentration difficult in the second examination paper. A subconscious doubt was nagging at my mental processes. And then, as I completed question three it suddenly surfaced. I pulled the bill and change from my jacket pocket. 'Sausages and mash, 2s 3d; Sultana pudding, 8d; Coffee 3d. Total 3s 2d.' There was 5s 10d in silver and copper.

And the shilling missing meant the loss of 20 cigarettes.

My copy of *'The Businessman's Guide to Britain.'* (The Economist Intelligence Unit: 1953) gives the following advice on tipping:

Restaurants – 10 per cent. 15 per cent.

Cloakrooms – 1s.

Chambermaid – 2s 6d per day.

Hairdresser – 20 per cent.

Hotel and Railway Porters – 1s per case (about).

Commissionaires – 1s.

Taxi Drivers – 20 per cent, (never less than 6d).

It says nothing, unfortunately, about tipping an American commissionaire six yards distant while you are struggling with the handle of a taxi door in a tropical storm; and it is significantly reticent about waiters who charge a shilling for helping you to read 'No Tips' backwards.

WATCH OUT FOR THE BOSS'S DAUGHTER

LOOKING along my shelves the other day I was amazed and somewhat ashamed to discover that I have more than forty books instructing me how to grow rich. The oldest of these manuals of self-help, *Making Your First £10,000*, cost me five shillings, and the author a Mr Jethro Pemberton, clearly hoped to sell the 400,000 copies that would net him his first £10,000 in royalties. If Pemberton had taken his own advice – the tips offered throughout his book – he'd have been broke by 1934, for the shares he recommended were all tobogganing in the shadow of a fearful economic slump.

In fact, only one of these books of mine was in any way helpful and that was a light-hearted little thing called *Riches Within Reach* containing advice of a flippant, jesting nature. Here are a few of its maxims:

The quickest way to the top is via the boss's daughter.

If the boss hasn't a daughter and you can't persuade him to adopt one,
then it might be a good idea to make the boss's wife your mistress.

If the boss isn't married, join his club and get to know him socially.

Rapid advancement is possible if you allow the boss to beat you
regularly at golf.

If he beats you by cheating, so much the better. Let him know that you
know about the sevens and eights recorded on his card as birdies and pars
and about the hole in his pocket through which he drops balls conveniently
near to the pin or conveniently free from the rough.

Avoid the boss's secretary unless she happens to be his daughter.

Nonsense of course, but a fair number of would-be tycoons
have made their play for the boss's daughter. Boofy Impringle
for example.

Boofy was a junior clerk with Senderton and Vestplacht,
stockbrokers, and his chances of promotion were negligible in
spite of his bogus Old Etonian tie, four 'O' levels and member-
ship of the Bunny Club. He was immensely ambitious and
spent most of his time in sycophantic attendance on Maurice
Senderton. Unfortunately, Senderton was blind to Boofy's
ministrations, unaware that his newspapers were carefully
ironed every morning, that fresh flowers appeared on his desk
and that his ashtrays were emptied dozens of times a day.

Nor was he aware that the young man who caddied for him
on Saturdays and Sundays at Westwich was a junior clerk in his
office, or that the man he saw polishing his Bentley so regularly
was a member of his clerical staff. For three years Boofy
laboured to win his master's approval and was completely
ignored.

Then he had a stroke of luck. He was working late at the
office one night when the phone rang and Senderton asked for
his secretary.

'I'm afraid Miss Dempster isn't here, sir,' said Boofy. 'This is
Impringle, sir. Can I be of service, sir?'

'Who *is* that?' barked Senderton.

'Impringle, sir. One of your clerks.'

'Impringle, eh. Well, there are some papers in my desk in a
file marked Carothers. Bring them to my flat in Redbury Mews.
You'll find the keys to my desk in Miss Dempster's cubby-hole.
And hurry!'

Impringle was thrilled. Fifteen minutes later he alighted
from a taxi and rang the bell of the flat. The door was opened by
a young lady in red slacks – a blonde – and Impringle stepped
past her and strode towards the sound of music. Senderton was
lying on a settee with a glass in his hand.

'What the !' he said. 'Who the devil are you?'

'Impringle, sir, with the papers.'

'You've been mighty quick, my boy. Thank you.' And he
held out his hand for the file.

'A pleasure, sir,' said Impringle. 'Lucky I was working late,
but then I usually do. So if ever you need anything at any time,
sir, I'm always on the job. Happy to be of service, sir.'

The blonde was now in the room. She poured whisky into a

cumbler. Impringle watched her and failed therefore to observe the boss's dismissive gesture. The blonde, also unobservant, handed Impringle the glass.

'Er, my daughter, Mary,' said Senderton. 'Mary, this is Impringle from the office.'

Impringle shook hands and his eyes lit up. He had remembered a line from *Riches Within Reach* – 'The quickest way to the top is via the boss's daughter.' His chance had come. His big chance. He sipped the whisky and looked into Mary's eyes.

Senderton rose, relieved Boofy of the glass and guided him to the door.

'Thank you again, Impringle,' he said. 'Collect the taxi fare from petty cash tomorrow. Goodnight.'

Impringle walked home, all the way to Cockfosters, in a dream, and during a sleepless, feverish night he laid his plans. There would be no more futile ironing of the boss's newspapers, no more car polishing . . . from now on he would lay siege to Redbury Mews and the heart of Mary Senderton.

His notions of gallantry were old-fashioned. He delivered flowers to the mews every morning. He called Mary on the phone and inquired politely about her health. He kept vigil outside the flat each evening, waiting for an opportunity to press his amorous suit in person.

'I'm not offering you weaponry, old boy – I'm offering you sophisticated weaponry.'

The reader will know by now that Impringle was a credulous fool. Yet his folly, mounting rapidly during the next few weeks, was to have an astonishing and totally unexpected effect on his career.

One dark night the door of the mews flat opened and Senderton appeared. He walked across to Boofy who raised his elbows to ward off an expected right swing.

'Hello, Impringle,' said Senderton genially, 'come and have a drink.'

Speechless, Boofy followed him into the flat. For 10 minutes or so Senderton was affable. Then he excused himself.

'I've got an appointment,' he said, 'but I know Mary will be safe in your hands. Plenty of booze in the cupboard. Enjoy yourselves.'

There were tears in Mary's eyes when Impringle made his first tentative advances. He was too stupid to understand their meaning and interpreted them as a tribute to his overpowering sex-appeal . . .

*   *   *

The asterisks represent a fortnight of passionate progress in Boofy's *affaire* with Mary.

In the office Senderton was now less boorish. Everyone remarked on it. He seemed rejuvenated, freed from an awkward burden. It was as though he had escaped from an embarrassing liaison.

And then, only a month after Boofy's first kiss, Senderton sent for him.

'I'm very pleased with you, Impringle,' he said. 'I like your work, and now a little bird tells me you're thinking of marrying and I'd like to give you a leg up. I'm promoting you to a head clerkship and if you keep your nose clean you'll be in line eventually for a partnership.'

Boofy stammered his thanks.

'And I hope you'll be happy with Mary. Nice girl, Mary Wilkinson, one of the best. I don't mind admitting that I rather fancy her myself, or did. But we haven't much chance, we older men, in competition with you young things. The better man has won, Impringle, and I don't bear any grudge.'

And as he shook Boofy's hand he winked.

The Impringle of Senderton, Vestplacht and Impringle, made good without marrying the boss's daughter. He is, of course, the author of the successful manual *How to Hit the Jackpot without Pull*.

PART 4
SHOPPING AND
ADVERTISING
MOSTLY

SHARING A MEAL WITH THE BOSS

A YOUNG business executive wrote to me the other day in something of a panic. He and his wife had been invited to a private dinner party at the home of his chairman, and he was worried about matters of etiquette. 'You see,' he wrote, 'we have lived such a Spartan existence since we married, three years ago, that we are scared of making fools of ourselves over a proper, slap-up, knife-and-fork, sit-down meal. Living out of tins and on sandwiches in order to rake together mortgage repayments is no sort of training for a session at the festive board of a tycoon, and I should be most grateful for any tips you can give me. My wife and I are particularly worried about soup, finger-bowls, bread, the proper use of cutlery, serviettes, cruet tipping and fish-bones.'

'We could, however, show a very small profit if the Conservatives were to return our contribution to party funds.'

Well, Jim (not his real name), I'll do my best. Table manners are not what they were, but the following principles still, I think, hold good.

1. You can create a good impression by lingering over your second or third cocktail and asking your host whether you might take it in to dinner with you. 'That young man,' thinks the host, 'is no lush,' and you are off to a good start.

2. Before you sit down make sure that the lady on your right is already seated. The approved method of helping a lady to be seated is for you to push the chair gently under her derriere. If the manoeuvre is executed too energetically the lady's rib-cage and possibly her pearls will suffer collision with the edge of the table, and you may spend an embarrassing five minutes on your knees looking for bits of equipment – buttons, beads, contact lenses – scattered in the mishap.

3. Place your napkin (not serviette, and never 'nappie') on your lap and try to forget about it. It will slip to the carpet and you will be tempted to retrieve it, but the temptation should be resisted, for the host will write off any male guest seen fumbling beneath the table as gauche, and the ladies on your flanks may view your activities with suspicion and, perhaps, alarm.

Do not tuck the napkin into your neck between collar and Adam's apple, and don't, however surreptitiously, wipe your nose with it.

4. Do not scribble figures or diagrams on the tablecloth. Businessmen often do this in restaurants and are, of course, charged an extra £1.50p for the fried potatoes or lettuce salad to cover laundry bills. But to disfigure a tablecloth in a private house is unforgivable.

5. The Boss will draw you into the general conversation as early as possible with a question about your last business trip to Glasgow or Frankfurt, and since you will assume that he is quizzing you about expenses your mind will be fully occupied.

6. Soup is drunk from the soup-spoon, which should collect the liquid as it (the spoon) moves *away* from the diner. The idea here is to allow soup to drip into the plate from the underside of the spoon on its return journey and not on to the napkin, trousers or shirt. For the same reason the plate should be tilted away from the diner when the soup is too shallow for comfortable spooning.

7. Try to keep the word 'pounds' down to minimum use in your conversation. Your hostess is probably an ambitious socialite who deplores any mention of filthy lucre at her board, and talk consisting of '. . . pounds . . . per cent . . . margin . . . profit . . . pounds . . . ' will automatically make you *persona non grata* in her little book.

8. The knife should *always* be held with the handle buried in the palm of the hand, and so should the fork when it is being used with the knife. Certain jumped-up and uncouth types hold the knife as they would a pen, and this practice is to be deprecated as strongly as possible – more strongly even than the effeminate display of the little finger when holding a teacup. The penholder grip is not only a reminder of 'shop' and clerkly origins; it is thoroughly inefficient.

9. The use of the cruet, while not prohibited, is not recommended. When mustard is 'runny' it can be kept in place on the rim of your plate behind an embankment of salt. Otherwise salt should be used sparingly and *never* scattered chipshop fashion.

10. It is difficult to offer sensible advice about the handling of fish bones, gristle and other inedible detritus. Some authorities recommend the collection of such matter in a cheek-pocket until the entire hoard can be deftly removed between thumb and finger. 'I think I've got a sixpence!' is possibly the best comment to make should you be scrutinised at the moment of extraction, and it should be accompanied by a light chuckle.

Don't refold your napkin for the next diner: leave it under the table. And don't *worry*.

HOW TO SUCCEED ON TV

I HAVE been reading the CBI guide for businessmen. 'Don't be afraid of the Box,' by Dr Bertram Mycock. The good doctor is anxious to improve the tycoon's image on television where it is all too easy to appear improperly dressed. It is a mistake, for example, to wear full evening dress when taking part in a debate on an industrial dispute. Why? Because your opponents and most viewers will fail to appreciate that the suit in question is the only presentable one you have, and will assume, incorrectly, that the debate is merely a disagreeable chore interrupting a night of extravagance and orgy.

'Don't wear horizontal stripes or pronounced checks,' says Dr Mycock. Fairly obvious advice, this. Horizontal stripes not only produce the optical illusion of obesity: they could be reminiscent of the uniform in which pop cartoonists dress the inhabitants of H.M. Prisons. As for loud checks, well, businessmen oughtn't to look like bookmakers, and the word check may possibly suggest its phonetic equivalent and filthy lucre.

Businessmen are urged not to fiddle – not even with a 'prestige gold propelling pencil' and any fool can see why. When I last appeared on the box, in the company of a trade union official and a down-at-heel economist, I was careful to discard all outward signs of affluence, my rings, gold bracelet, ear-rings and monogram tie-clip, and I rolled up my shirt-sleeves so that the camera could not zoom in on my MCC cuff-links. I was wearing a tuxedo because at the time I had a second job as relief wine waiter at 'The Turtle Soup' off Regent Street, and not wishing to upstage my debating colleagues I fitted the dinner jacket with leather elbow and cuff patches. This, I was told by the producer, was a mistake. 'You can't fool viewers with tricks like that,' he said.

If you *must* fiddle with something, make it something ordinary and proletarian – a screwdriver, perhaps, the clasp on your braces or a very cheap ball-point. A friend of mine achieved instant success on TV when he was interviewed with a dog collar in his hand. Viewers are, of course, mad about dumb animals and their heart went out to a man who had either lost his dog or was waiting to get home to fit Rover with new neckwear.

Even more important than appearance is the businessman's delivery. 'Don't flannel,' says Dr Mycock. Yes, and when the anchor man puts his first question to you don't start with 'Before I answer that question may I say . . . ' and go on to deliver a speech you have learned parrot-fashion. Nothing infuriates viewers more than this tiresome gambit unless it's the wretched habit of interrupting an opponent before he's completed his first sentence with 'Look, fair's fair, you've had your turn: I listened patiently to what you had to say, but it's my turn now so please let me finish what *I* have to say. No I insist, we don't want a slanging match, but I'm as much entitled as you to state my views.'

A lot of businessmen are incorrigibly vain. Invited to appear in 'Nationwide' at six o'clock they turn up at about three and ask immediately for the make-up room. Nowadays TV cosmetics for panelists and debaters are usually restricted to a quick dab of powder on the highlights of the forehead, and it is a mistake to ask the make-up girls for eye-shadow, lipstick and patches of artificial hair.

On the other hand, one can *floor* an adversary – in fact all present – by attempting an unusual manoeuvre during a debate. A year or so ago, when Harrison Sidewhistle, managing director of a Runcorn glue company, was taking part in a high-powered discussion on the Common Market it soon became apparent that he was outclassed. The question-master, Robin Day, I think, was trying to help Harrison overcome his nervousness when the panellist suddenly switched on a battery-driven razor and began to smooth away his five o'clock shadow.

Instantly, the balance of the programme changed to Sidewhistle's advantage. The camera zoomed in on his features while Day and the other debaters were struck dumb. This gimmick was a huge success and for several months afterwards producers clamoured for Harrison Sidewhistle's services.

I am rather surprised that Dr Mycock fails to mention the battery-operated razor in his guide.

ARE WE BECOMING A NATION OF HOTEL-KEEPERS?

UNLIKE many financial pundits I believe that British hotels are soon to enjoy a major boom. For several years now, while investment in manufacturing industry has been sluggish, the Government and private enterprise have pumped vast sums into hotel construction. Our holiday accommodation has therefore expanded to meet all possible demands.

So our hotels will be able to meet a huge increase in the number of travellers from the Continent (international meetings of trade unionists, sociologists and industrial consultants), a possible annual influx of 3,000 Asians and Africans holding British passports, refugees from Malta, Gibraltar, Australia and Canada, IRA officials and militant sympathisers, thousands of American newsmen anxious to sight Howard Hughes, missionaries from China, hot-gospellers from the Middle West, and onion-sellers from Brittany.

Our own people, I regret to say, will not be able to afford to stay in these new hotels, but by working diligently in them as porters, waiters, chambermaids, chip-chefs and shoe-cleaners they should earn enough to manage a fortnight in their old stamping grounds on the Costa Brava and in Majorca.

Hollowood

'I've invited you here, Smythe, because I'd like to discuss the insurance of our fleet of 4,000 electric milk vans and my son's sports car with you.'

The British make marvellous hoteliers. We understand servility better than the Americans, who have some difficulty in enunciating the terms 'please' and 'thank you' (though, curiously enough, they are good at 'you're welcome'). The Americans are reputedly slick and economical, yet they can label a hotel door 'Not an Accredited Egress' when they mean 'No Exit'; and they can infuriate guests in need of air by confronting them with the notice 'This window has been sealed in the interest of hotel visitors: do not try to adjust.'

Are British hotels ahead of those on the Continent? I think so. Our television programmes are better, so that time seems to pass much more quickly when one is waiting for room service or while the water in the bathroom is reaching a temperature suitable for shaving. Our service is discreet. In British hotels foreigners can speak freely in their own language without fear of eavesdroppers. Our hotel staff is monoglot, if that, and converses with guests only in hand-signs of which the most common is the palm face-upwards and at right angles to an arm held rigidly to attention.

British food is excellent. On the Continent breakfast usually consists of croissants and coffee, a poor substitute for our traditional porridge, eggs and bacon, toast and marmalade, and those rock-hard foreign rolls are obviously a poor substitute for our delicious sliced bread each piece of which is as flat – and I mean flat – as the cloth on a billiards table.

With a good British breakfast inside him the visitor can consider other hotel meals with equanimity. Lunch and dinner are obviously OK because they are printed in French, and afternoon tea is really another breakfast with teacakes or crumpets deputising for the eggs and bacon.

At the end of the day, during which the Continental visitor has bought two or three British businesses and the American has helped himself to a sector of North Sea oil, there is the ritual – unknown outside Britain – of 'seeing the night porter.' This friendly soul offers you a ball-point and a ledger in which you are invited to write your room number and a series of dots.

These instruct the hotel to awaken you, like the person in Room 732, at 7.30 with a pot of tea and copies of the *Daily Telegraph* and the *Daily Express*. Next morning, dead on eight o'clock, you get your tea as planned together with the *Times* and the *Daily Mail*.

Try to obtain this service in New York and punctually at 5.30 a.m the door of your room will splinter under the weight of a single copy of the *New York Times* hurled by a bell-hop. Try it on the Continent and you will be lucky to get a cup of lukewarm soda-water, a bag containing tea made from acorns and a copy of yesterday's *Le Monde*.

There is no tipping in British hotels. You pay a service charge of 15 p.c., and that's that if you remember that people who open your car door, carry anything for you or look at you in a certain way expect a suitable contribution to their tax-free income.

Above all, the British hotel is friendly. In certain parts of the hotel, known as public bars, the British themselves may be seen. Visitors should take advantage of this opportunity to *mix* and escape from the fellow-foreigners with whom they have to rub shoulders in lifts, corridors, dining rooms and lounges.

Though poor, the British will readily respond if you offer them a drink. They will probably delight you by pretending to speak your language, by cursing the Common Market, French farming policy and Germany's weak-kneed trade unions, and by recounting their memoirs of one or two world wars. If they try to tell you a joke it is best to laugh when they do and reply with something like 'Ah, you English and your incomparable sense of humour!'

If this is said with enough conviction they may, conceivably, offer to buy *you* a drink though if you dawdle they will amost certainly say they have to get back to the office before you've had time to accept.

While you are buying British businesses or acquiring the North Sea you may be entertained to lunch by a native – or rather by his company, generously assisted by the Commissioners of Inland Revenue. This is quite an occasion for the Englishman since it gives him a rare opportunity to eat the traditional English roast beef.

If there is an 'R' in the month, and your host is in the clear with his company's accountant, you will probably start with oysters. He will then make a jocular reference to their supposedly aphrodisiac properties. But the beef is the *pièce de résistance*, as the natives say and the British, suspicious of substitutes, like to see as much as possible of the animal they are about to eat.

A heated trolley trundles to your table and your host emits an appreciative 'aah!' as the lid is lifted from a colossal salver. The beef carver smiles throughout his task of slicing up the carcase. Your host will unceremoniously slip a coin or a note into his hand, the sum depending on the size of the helpings.

Should you, as a visitor, wish to sample the Briton's normal fare then enter his local pub. There you will be able to eat the sandwich, which had an earl named after it; the pickled onion; and the banger or pork and bread sausage. By the way, the English can't afford whisky so if you ask for 'a scotch' in a pub you may get an ancient egg with a coating of sausage meat cemented round it. And you will eat it, or try to, standing up.

Yes, all visitors should experience British pubs, if only more fully to appreciate the fantastic improvement in our booming, or about to boom, hotel industry.

THE TRUTH ABOUT DO-IT-YOURSELF MARKETING

WHEN the chairman of the National Housebuilders Registration Council said the other day that houses would be somewhat cheaper if they were sold unfinished I thought he was joking. He wasn't. Sir Stanley Morton was making the first verbal move in yet another battle against inflation. Soon the builders will be joined by manufacturers and we'll be told, we consumers, that prices are ridiculously high merely because we insist on buying goods ready for use.

Many furniture makers have already recognised the fact that ordinary breadwinners can no longer afford to buy desks, kitchen cabinets, stools, chairs and tables the way their parents bought them. So they offer us bundles of wood and wire complete with neat little booklets called 'Assembling the LR 1099 Bedside Table' or 'The Brinkwood Piano Co., Baby Grand, Manual of Assembly.' And it won't be long. I think, before we are all expected to accept delivery of a new car, washing machine or colour TV set in easyfit parts. Oh, yes, I can see it coming, and I don't like the look of it.

Some husbands revel in assembly jobs and finishing routines. They get a kick out of the work and are never happier than when demonstrating to me how simple it is to knock up an outhouse or a patio with the aid of one of these marvellous electrically-driven power tools. And when I tell them that I consider adhesive tape the only true friend of the handyman manqué they scoff. Let them.

Of course it can be argued that the do-it-yourself movement really started in the arts when chaps like Picasso offered us canvases strewn with eyes, ears, birds and breasts and invited us to assemble the components into anything we had a mind to fancy. And I'm pretty certain that composers such as Stockhausen, Cage and Birtwhistle are on to a good thing, or think they are, when they dish out the decibels wholesale and expect listeners to fit them together to make comprehensible music.

All right, I'm a philistine totally lacking in aesthetic sensibility. And OK, I'm old-fashioned economically when I confess that I prefer goods as ready for instant use as modern packaging allows to goods that are merely loose collections of spare parts.

I could retaliate by offering unfinished essays instead of the reasoned and finely honed prose customarily featured in this column. It would save me a lot of time to write 'Unfinished Money-Go-Round Article. Please assemble from the following words: the (25), money (6), a (27), long, fortune, bread, common, gross, in (12), profits (3), unnecessary, turbulent, however, now (2), breakfast, and (27), moreover, secondly, engaging, captain, of (6) go (2), Keynes, making, Tuesday (5), never . . . to form an interesting piece on some topic of the hour. Words selected by Bernard Hollowood.'

A few months ago my wife drew my attention to the fact that the desk in my study was past its best. For some time I had experienced strange sensations when writing at it: sometimes the paper would give under my pen so that I seemed to be operating on an eiderdown, and there were occasions when the nib was lost to view in the depths of a depression. My wife explained that the wooden surface of the desk had perished leaving the covering of old leather without support and rather like a trampoline.

'Maybe it's not quite as solid as it was when we inherited it from your grandfather,' I said, 'but it will see me out. There are still thousands of articles and reviews in that old desk.'

'But it's dangerous,' she said, 'positively lethal. One of these fine days, when you're underlining or pressing on just a little too hard with your descenders (I write copperplate, always have) you'll go clean through that leather and there'll be a nasty accident. Don't be so mean! You need a new desk. Let's go to Debbridges and get one.'

The desk I finally bought was a lulu, a glorious piece of Bauhaus-style modernity in wet-look enamels. And the price wasn't bad either – a mere £179.99.

It arrived together with the invoice only a fortnight later. It was delivered by British Rail in a cardboard box about four feet square and nine inches deep upon which was stencilled the message 'The Slater Executive Desk. See inside for "Jiffy" Assembly Guide.'

Needless to say, I was furious. There had been no mention of the 'Jiffy' when I had inspected the furnitue in Debbridges palatial showrooms. Knowing that I should prove unequal to the task of fitting the bits together, I wanted to send them back, but my wife pointed out that having paid a deposit of £17 on the desk and signed a purchasing agreement I was in honour bound to make a go of the transaction.

So I engaged the services of a local joiner, and together we knocked up a fair imitation of the Slater Executive. We had only one drawer and two lengths of hardboard surplus to requirements when the deed was done though the desk turned out to be a foot lower than expected and more than four feet longer.

And so as I near the end of this article I am suffering from acute backache though otherwise perfectly happy with my riposte to Debbridges. What I did, after much thought, was to send them 24 sheets of 2p stamps, 73 postal orders for amounts varying from 20p to £3.37, four money orders, 2,826 ½p pieces, an assortment of old sixpences and half-crowns, an IOU for £14.23, a bundle of very shabby pound notes and a covering note reading: 'Please assemble the enclosed into £162.99, being balance owing on purchase of Slater Executive Desk.'

Childish? I suppose so. But I feel we've got to hit back somehow.

BLUE BATS AND THE NEW ADVERTISING

A SHOP in New York once tried to sell me a wall-clock with the letters ATIMINCCLOCK instead of numerals. I was horrified, and said so.

'It's real cheap,' said the salesman, 'only 59 bucks.'

'Look,' I said, 'even if you paid *me* 59 dollars to advertise your Timinc clocks with this monstrosity I wouldn't give it house room.'

He couldn't understand my objection. 'You buy a Caddy or a Chevvy with the name plastered all over it,' he said, 'so what's the difference?'

I told him that many people object to the flamboyant branding of consumer durables such as cars, TV sets, freezers, radio and so on.

'I buy a car,' I said, 'and it's *mine*, so what right has the manufacturer to stick *his* name all over it and to stencil "This is a Thunderbolt 1984, a product of the Nitcrick Foundation" in white paint all over the rear window. Colossal cheek, if you ask me.

'Mind you I've no objection to discreet nameplates. Potters as distinguished as Wedgwood, Royal Worcester and Crown Derby wouldn't dream of including their monickers in the design or pattern of a plate: they sign their names with a backstamp on the underside of the vessel. And the same goes for tailors and hatters – a neat label on the inside of a coat or trilby. How would you like it if your suit carried the tailors name in large letters on the breast pocket?'

I'd said the wrong thing, for he grinned and pointed to the lapels of his light-blue jacket both of which bore the device 'There's no tick-tock like a Timinc Clock' in yellow letters in a green circle.

'Oh, well.' I said, 'that's different. That's a working jacket and the property of your employer. I'm talking about a *private* suit, civvies.'

'I guess you Limeys are different,' he said. 'I hear you don't have commercials on your TV over there, and I guess that's on account of your being commies or as near as damn it.'

I explained about the BBC and the IBA and told him we have strict regulations about the content of TV advertisements.

'So I guess your IBA wouldn't allow a jingle for coffins, eh? Year or two back we had one that went . . . *Casey coffins they are fine, made of satin, brass and pine; and when death knocks at your door, phone Columbus 204*. A real killer that, better than the Jack Benny show.'

Well, what I'm gradually getting round to is the affair of the coloured cricket bats. Clever advertisers manage to grab themselves a lot of free advertising on TV – even on BBC TV. At Wimbledon practically every tennis racket is blazoned with the initial of the manufacturer: not a minute trademark on the handle but a huge letter S (for Slazenger), D (for Dunlop) or whatever right *across the strings*. I wonder who thought that one up, and whether he's now in affluent retirement on the proceeds of his brainwave?

In my day cricket bats all looked alike from the boundary, though legends such as 'Gunn and Moore, Nottingham. Specially Selected' and 'Philip Mead Autograph' were usually inscribed near the shoulder of the blade. Then came TV and the zoom lens and close-up studies of county cricketers in action: and bats became miniature hoardings.

One manufacturer marked his willow with a thick black stripe extending from handle to hump, and another, even more daring, faced his bat with a large black-and-white facial portrait of Basil D'Oliveira. Thousands of schoolboys and club cricketers took notice and rushed off to buy the weapons wielded by their heroes. A pity about the ball: it's too small to carry telegenic ads.

Then along came colour TV and new opportunities. For 200 years and more cricket bats have been wood coloured – white when new, but sometimes stained to the colour of a piano by repeated dosing with linseed oil, mud, dust, sweat (transferred via the ball from bowlers' foreheads) and the droppings of woodworm. It was time, some manufacturer thought, for a *change*. So last summer bats began to appear in all the colours of the spectrum. Barry Richards used an orange bat in a John Player League match, Graham Roope promised to use a blue bat in a Test. And the MCC got cold feet and banned chromatic willow until further notice.

I am sorry about this. Cricket *needs* more colour. To my knowledge no county cricketer has ever appeared in shorts even on the hottest day, and only the boys of Rugby School, who wear blue cricket shirts, have ever departed from the conventional white, cream or off-white cricketing garb. If I had my way, the cricket ball would be white, like most tennis balls, and far more readily visible to spectators and viewers; flannels and shirts would be in club colours, and stumps would be covered with percussive caps that would explode with a real bang when struck by the ball.

Mind you, I can see the MCC's point. If we give the manufacturers a free hand with bats they'll produce weapons (for openers) faced with rough sandpaper or broken glass and guaranteed to remove 'the shine' within one over.

I used to think that the more reticent a company in matters of advertising the brighter were its share prospects. I invested in a certain magazine because it spent nothing on advertising and spent its money instead on increasing the paper's girth and improving its literary content. And I backed Rolls-Royce very largely because it refused to plaster its motor vehicles with showy lettering and made do with a modest RR.

'No, dear, the Government's propensity to subsidize does not extend to the Stock Market.'

What finally changed my mind was my experience as an author. My first books sold well, but I didn't care for the brash manner in which they were advertised. So I found a new publisher who considered advertising a waste of money. My next book's one and only edition was heavily remaindered.

I am now at work on an economics text-book for 'O'-level students and every other page will consist of adverts. You'd be surprised how many manufacturers of potato crisps, iced lollies, choc bars, comics, pop records, false eyelashes, soccer scarves, soccer toilet rolls, itching powder, acne remover and horoscopes will pay really big money to reach the kids these days. I'm not saying that my idea is particularly ethical, but I'm assured of a fat profit before I've sold a single copy.

Even before I've put pen to paper.

THE ART OF SHOPPING AROUND

EVER since the abolition of Resale Price Maintenance we've been urged to 'shop around.' According to the Government, shopping around is the way to beat inflation or, if that seems rather a tall order, make the best of a terrifying price situation.

My father, I recall, managed to find bargains even in the days of fixed prices, but my father will have to wait his turn like everyone else in this article.

The discerning, discriminating shopper, we are told, always buys in the cheapest market, which means that she (or he) keeps tabs on all the stores within reasonable shopping distance and all the changes in price from week to week or, if possible, from day to day. Well, this is good advice if you happen to own a computer and are prepared to make shopping a full-time business, but for most people it is just not on. I've tried it. Correction, my wife has.

A year or two ago I lectured her on the stupidity of supermarket shopping. 'What's the use of Heath and Barber telling us to shop around,' I said, 'if you buy all our week's groceries in one fell swoop at Finchmarket? There are a dozen supermarkets in Cribbleigh, all charging different prices for the same goods!'

'I know,' she said, 'but what can I do about it? It takes me the best part of a morning to park the car fairly near to Finchmarket, do the rounds, queue for ages at the cash points, lug the stuff to the car, argue with a traffic warden and get home in time to cook your lunch. How the hell could I get round *twelve* supermarkets?'

'Steady on!' I said. 'I'm only trying to be helpful.'

'I've tried Tesco and PB Stores' she said, 'and a week's shopping comes to roughly the same beastly amount in each. Finchmarket is cheaper for some things, dearer for others, and so are Tesco and PB. Theoretically, I could save at least a pound a week by buying all the loss leaders, but in practice I should spend more than that on parking fees and shoe-leather, and never have a moment to call my own. And, of course, I shouldn't be able to do your typing: you'd have to hire a secretary.'

I look back on the days before 1962, when RPM was in operation, as a golden age. I could pop into a shop anywhere in the country, plonk down my six bob (or whatever) and get my ounce of Old Friar rough cut. Every shop had to charge the same price. Had to! The little shop on the corner, the department store, the chain store, the supermarket. It was great!

I went shopping with my father only once. He held the views, surprising in a Conservative who worshipped Stanley Baldwin, that all shopkeepers were rogues and profiteers, and that shopping was essentially a war of nerves between shopkeeper and customer.

A month or two after starting work I announced my intention of buying a new coat. This was quite a moment – the first time I had spent my own money on something more substantial than sweets or comics. My father lowered his newspaper, removed his pipe from his mouth and said 'I'll come with you. You don't buy overcoats every day and unless you understand cloth they'll make you pay through the nose.'

In my innocence I thanked him.

Hallowood

'Have a scout round, there's a good chap, and see if you can spot a few more invisible exports.'

We marched into one of the smartest gents' outfitters in the town, a small establishment run by the owner, a Mr Nazeby, and two assistants, and asked to see winter overcoats. Mr Nazeby led us to a rack and invited me to study the contents. Almost immediately my eye settled on a gorgeous garment made of heavy worsted. It was brown with a subdued check pattern, a belt of the same material and wide lapels. I'd seen Leslie Howard sporting something similar at the Roxy two days before and I was as good as sold.

I said I liked it and Nazeby congratulated me on my choice. My father examined the fabric very carefully, and pronounced it serviceable. It fitted perfectly.

'How much is it?' I said anxiously.

Nazeby pretended not to know. He fished inside the coat's ticket pocket and extracted a rectangular card bearing coded markings.

'Six guineas, sir,' he said, and the "sir" was followed instantly by a piercing 'Phew!' from my father.

'I'll take it,' I said.

'You're not going to pay six pounds for a coat off the peg!' said my father. 'Are you out of your mind? Offer him five!'

Mr Nazeby chuckled. 'I'm sorry, sir,' he said, 'but the price is six guineas, and, if I may say so, very reasonable at that.'

'Nonsense!' said my father. 'The boy's paying cash. I know something about the tailoring business and in my experience tailors usually have to *wait* for their money. Five pounds would mean a discount of only a quid. Do yourself a favour, Nazeby, and snap the boy's hand off.'

Nazeby coloured a little, a mild pink to my puce, and his brows furrowed.

'Tell you what I'll do,' he said. 'I'll reduce it to six pounds, and that will mean saying good-bye to my profit.'

'Make it five guineas,' said my father, 'and you've sold a coat.'

I didn't know where to put myself. I was deeply ashamed. This was my own father and he was a huckster and obviously enjoying himself. Nazeby looked thoroughly uncomfortable.

'I don't think you realise, sir,' he said, 'what a splendid coat this is. I know six pounds sounds a lot, but I can assure you your son's got a real bargain.'

'Very well,' said my father, 'five guineas it is. You'd better wrap it up.'

I thought Nazeby would explode. He stood irresolute for 10 seconds or so, then slowly shook his head and began to write out the bill.

My father smirked at me.

'You've got a good coat there,' he said. 'Worth every penny of five pounds.'

Nazeby looked up and there was a glint of hardened steel in his eye.

'Five guineas,' he said, 'and that's my final offer!'

I busied myself writing out the cheque. Slowly the atmosphere improved, and my father saw fit to introduce new topics into the conversation – the weather and the doings of the City football club – as Nazeby prepared to make a neat parcel of the coat.

My father timed his move to perfection. He waited until Nazeby was near the end of the packing, until the brown paper needed only one more fold to cover the coat. Then he whipped a couple of ties off a rack on the counter, prodded them into the parcel and turned to me.

'I'm sure Mr Nazeby won't grudge you a tie,' he said, 'when you're spending so much in his shop.'

Nazeby completed the parcel, accepted the cheque and uttered a frigidly polite: 'Good evening, gentlemen!'

'I've never been so humiliated in my life!' I said as soon as we were in the street. 'Really, father!'

'You'll learn,' he said. 'If you don't stand up for yourself, shopkeepers will rook you. Those ties should just about do the trick. That coat's worth a fiver and not a penny more.'

I never went shopping with him again. He didn't like RPM, but I shudder to think how he'd react to today's advice of 'Shop around.'

DISCOUNT, THE ROOT OF ALL EVIL

ONE WAY of insulating oneself from the major economic worries of the day is to focus all one's animosity upon a relatively minor flaw in the commercial scene. If you can't bear to look at the list of market prices, to contemplate the programme outlined in the White Paper on The Regeneration of British Industry, or to brood on the possibility of a bloody clash between the unions and para-military organisations of middle-class chauvinists, I suggest that you find some minor grouse and give full rein to it.

Our capacity for passion is limited and to bellyache enthusiastically about a relatively insignificant matter can, I find, free one from the incubus of more desperate rumination.

I'm not going to tell you which of the innumerable surrogate worries are most worthwhile. In this business it's every man for himself. But I can tell you that before settling on discount prices as my little *bête noir* I gave a lot of consideration to (1) football hooliganism, (2) the reduction in the number of trainee teachers, (3) the middle-order batting of the team to tour Australia, (4) the price of commemorative coin issues, (5) the Osmonds and tenny-boppers, (6) keg bitter, (7) the next wage-claim by the NUM, (8) Gerald Ford, (9) the £50 I have in tax-reserve certificates which are earning no interest and (10) the rumoured melting of the polar ice-caps.

I settled on discount prices when I was showing off my new stereo record player to guests.

'Oh, you've got an Andectex, too!' said Larry Maitland, downing his first gin-and-tonic in one and eyeing the gin bottle. 'Cheapest buy on the market. Well, you won't regret it: ours is terrific, total fidelity.'

'Not exactly cheap though,' I said. 'At least, *I* don't call £165 cheap.'

'£165?' said Larry. 'Surely you didn't pay the manufacturer's recommended price? We got ours for £125 through the Landed Gentry Society and I believe I've seen them in Dixon's Discount Mart for £120.'

My evening was completely ruined and I was sorely tempted to water the gin and apologise after supper for running out of brandy.

When the Maitlands had left I noticed that my wife seemed somewhat down in the mouth.

'I'm sorry,' I said, 'if I embarrassed you with the one about the Greek Orthodox Church. It just slipped out.'

'It's not that,' she said, 'but Rosie Maitland was telling me they've just paid £202 for a ride-on lawnmower, a Crampion, the same model exactly that we paid £250 for six months ago. She laughed at me when I told her what ours cost.'

'I suppose they got that through their precious Landed Gentry Society, too,' I said.

'No, they didn't. They got it from Perkins's like us. Apparently, it was marked at £250 and Larry told them he could get the identical machine through the firm at £200. So they settled finally for £202 including delivery.'

'Through the firm?' I said. 'Larry's with Shell. How on earth could Shell have any pull with a lawnmower manufacturer?'

'Search me!' my wife said, 'but it made me feel quite ill to think we'd been such suckers.'

Well, after that I checked on all our purchases and discovered to my horror that we were paying through the nose for practically everything. Before the Budget I spent an hour comparison shopping for my favourite brand of cigarettes and returned triumphantly with 200 at 36p per 20, and a day or two later in 'The Grapes' heard Nobby Eastleigh say that he never paid more than 34p at a cut-price stores in Kingston.

Now it could be that this appalling inequality is at the root of social unrest in Britain. We have become a nation of us and them – us being the poor dopes who pay something like the manufacturer's recommended price, and them being the smarty-pants who pay substantially less. Do they (them) realise that they are being subsidised by us? And do they realise that their commercial capers are contributing to the friction between classes that could explode into active hostility?

People opposed to any move towards equality of distribution accuse the egalitarians of being inspired by envy, and they may be right. But no one in his right mind objects to equality of opportunity, and there's very little of this when one group has the market rigged in such a way that its members obtain nearly all their goods on preferential terms.

In theory, of course, there's nothing to prevent a miner from becoming a member of the Landed Gentry Society, the City and Suburban Discount Trust or the Gentlefolk Purchasing Association, but I doubt very much whether more than 1 p.c. of Joe Gormley's lads have even heard of these organisations. On the other hand I doubt whether a single member of these organisations is unaware of the miner's free ration of coal – if you see what I mean.

What would happen, I wonder, if the employees of GLS International made it a condition of their service that they should enjoy the same rights as the directors and top executives to buy personally 'through the firm' on advantageous terms?

And what about the pensioner? Why should a retired executive have to pay much more for consumer durables than the man on full pay?

I'm all for equality of opportunity even if it would mean sacrificing the five *free* magazines I receive by post every week.

IT AYS TO DVERTISE

ADVERTISING MEN, with whom I sometimes sip an iced lolly, are enthusiastic about the recent breakthrough in technique by 'you know who.' For many years the distinguished company that produces (well, why not, I'm not on the BBC) Schweppes tonic water has been cunningly reluctant to yell the name from the house-tops. It preferred to whisper it with a telling and enticing sibilance, allowing only fragments of its lettering to appear in pictorial advertisements.

Well 'you know who' have gone one better with the dramatic rediscovery of the virtues of abbreviation. Almost overnight the familiar 'Sch' or 'Ssssch' has been relegated to second place and the product that goes naturally with gin is being plugged as 'Weppes.' Astonishing! The public has been taken by storm by this dashing innovation and City types among Mayfair's 'in' crowd are ordering gin 'n Weppes with knowing and lofty superiority.

'What on earth am I looking in here for — the cigarettes are right in front of us on the desk?'

Of course this isn't the last we've heard of the Cadbury-Schweppes brainwave. Only last week at 'The Cellar' in York Passage I heard a handsome Guards officer ask for a 'vodka and Epps' and the wits of 'Meg's Place' and 'Hatches Down' are already puzzling bartenders and bunnies with orders for ' 'in 'n 'onic.'

You start something and there's always someone who wants to carry it to ridiculous extremes; and don't think your competitors will take this kind of thing lying down. I'm quite sure someone will shortly come up with Anada Dry and Tone's Inger Ales.

Abbreviation is not a mere sales gimmick. Its economic advantages are legion. Every schoolboy knows the value of a mnemonic and a clever crib, just as millions of readers prefer to make the acquaintance of the Bard through 'Lamb's Tales from Shakespeare' rather than from the folio texts. And let's not forget that the world's largest-selling magazine is *Reader's Digest*, with its condensed versions of literary exercises and masterpieces. I shall watch the bookseller's face closely when I ask him for a copy of the *Eader's Igest*.

Trade names are now so important that they can no longer be left to the entrepreneur. There are people in all the world's major cities who specialise in the nomenclature of clubs, committees, authorities, organisations, corporations and companies, and those responsible for floating one of these bodies can't afford to ignore the services offered.

The other day I was chatting to Osbert Kenneth Evans (Oke, of course, to his friends) who runs the firm of NAMIT, a title wooed from the initials of the ridiculous words Natural Alliance of Men in Themes. Oke maintains that there would be little interest in disarmament if the Americans had failed to boil down talks on strategic arms limitation to SALT.

'It's a great neologism,' he said, 'unforgettable, spicy and essential. The chap who devised it may have saved the world! It's probably too late now, but I should dearly like to have a go at CBI and TUC, which are terrible initials for organisations on which our economic future depends.'

'They seem all right to me,' I said. 'Simple and reasonably memorable. How could they be improved?'

He laughed. 'Well, if the Confederation and the Congress had consulted me in the first place,' he said, 'I could have given them initials with genuine appeal. CBI ought to be BOSS – say Board Of Super Superiors – or EMP (short for employers) from Excellent Master Producers. Don't you agree that BOSS or EMP would be infinitely more suitable than CBI?'

'Perhaps so,' I said. 'What about TUC?'

'Difficult to say off the cuff. How about TOIL, the Organisation of Island Labour?'

He went on to tell me how much he approved of Colin Cowdrey's old man for giving his cricketing son the initials MCC and how much better GG would be than Tote, GG standing apparently for General Gamble.

Inevitably we went on to consider quoted shares. He thought very little of most of the names and abbreviations. BATS and IMPS seemed irrelevant, though he thought Reed a respectable title for a company flogging paper, and Ass Paper terrible.

'We're moving into an age of multinationals,' he said, 'and we're kept pretty busy with combines, mergers and takeovers. Some of the names we've got really are marvellous. The Independent Rubber Empire (TIRE) for a rubber conglomerate. Central Automobile Research (CAR) for the next major motor merger. The Original Tipple (TOT) for combining distillers, General Retail Union Britain (GRUB) for the next super supermarket. Private Reorganisation of Independent News Traders (PRINT) for the big amalgamation in Fleet Street, World of Women (WOW) for a respectable sex shop, and so on.

We're just waiting for industry and the City to catch up with us.'

'Aren't you exaggerating?' I said. 'Investors can remember shares like ICI, Lonrho, Vehicle and General, Tate and Lyle without much trouble. I don't see the appeal of your TOT and GRUB.'

'Then you know very little about the common man. D'you ever look at the pages of car registration numbers wanted and on offer, and at the price some motorist is prepared to pay for the equivalent of NAB 1 or SEX 007? What's in a name? Everything. What is the registration number of *your* car?'

'CG . . . something. Oh, I forget. There's an 8 in it and I'm pretty sure it ends in 3.'

'Wouldn't it be more convenient if it were TEL 1973 or RIP 1984?'

'Yes, I suppose so, but . . .'

'Of course, I'm right!' he said. 'I'd like to bet that your portfolio is full – without your knowing it – of shares with initials that appeal to you subconsciously.'

'Really!' I said, starting to lose patience.

'Very well,' he said. 'Which are your companies?'

'British Alliance Investment Ltd . . .'

'Excellent!' he said. 'Carry on!'

'Pawson Abcock Diesel, Roscoe Union National, Brewster Amalgamated Leather Luggage, British Axminster Trust, Slater Thompson Underwear Mining Pumps, Charles . . .'

'Hold it!' he said. 'It's just as I thought. Your portfolio reveals your passion for cricket. Every investment is meaningful. Look at the initials BAIL, PAD, RUN, BALL, BAT, STUMP. And I shouldn't be surprised if the one beginning with Charles . . .'

'By golly, you're right!' I said. 'Incredible! The "Charles" investment is in fact the Charles Russell Inkpen and Cyril Kennedy Engineering Trust or . . .'

'Exactly!' he said. 'I knew it!'

LOW DOWN ON PRICE RISES

I HAVE been looking into this price adjustment business in the shops and I am happy to record that this aspect of inflation can't be blamed entirely on rascally, profiteering retailers. At Hyam's the grocer in the High Street, I drew attention of Rex Pendlebury, assistant manager, to a can of baked beans marked progressively at 3½p, 4p, 5½p, 7p and 9p. (The manager, a Mr Foxall, was indisposed with a stomach disorder caused by the ingestion of too much gum.)

'Ah,' said Pendlebury, blushing slightly, 'I can explain all that. You see, we sold the beans originally at 3½p as a loss leader. Then the manufacturers cut our supplies and we went up to 4p. About a fortnight ago a man we'd "planted" at Tesco reported their beans to be selling at 6p so we upped ours to 5½p; and a day or two later we noticed that women were beginning to hoard beans, and to preserve our stocks we had to mark the cans up to 7p. Then yesterday we found ourselves very short of labels of practically every denomination. There's an acute paper shortage and our suppliers are on a three-day week. I made a careful inventory of all the labels in stock and discovered that while we were right out of 7½ps, 8ps and 8½ps we still had a reasonable quantity of 6ps, 9ps and 11½ps.

'I had little choice then, did I? We'd managed to get a small delivery of baked beans from Somaliland and I could price them at either 9p or 11½p. And since I'd already earmarked the latter for meat pies, increased from 8p, I had no option but to use the 9p labels on the beans. Clear, squire?'

'It beats me,' I said, 'why you don't remove the old labels when you up the price. Nothing upsets customers more than the evidence of repeated inflationary changes.'

'Agreed, squire,' he said, 'but we have to use very firmly-stuck labels and it would take ages to chisel them all off besides leaving tell-tale toolmarks on the cans. A year ago we tried Ezeestik labels and had no end of trouble with customers. They'd pick up a tin, packet or jar, scrape off the top label, put the purchase into their trolley basket and hope to deceive the girls at the check-out points. So a firm bonding gum is absolutely essential.

'Course, that doesn't stop some customers trying to cheat. A company called Figaro Brothers now markets a do-it-yourself pack of labels in all prices, colours, shapes and sizes, and its dead easy for shoppers to stick their own price on goods taken from the shelves. More often than not they get away with it because the cash register operators are always in a frantic hurry. But sometimes the customer is too greedy and gets caught. Had a woman in last week – respectable middle-class lady with a chauffeur-driven Jaguar – who tried to pass off a joint marked at £2.49 as only 30p. Her label was exactly like ours, pale blue figures on a yellow ground. Her case comes up next month.'

'Some people claim,' I said, 'that decimalisation is responsible for a lot of supermarket inflation. Is that true in your case?'

'Not here, squire. It's too obvious. But I make a weekly tour of our competitors and some of 'em are brazen about it. I mean, in Faremart you can still see 1s 5d changed to 15p and 2s 6d altered to 26p, and I've even seen 1s 11d doctored to look like 111p! That's what I call real profiteering!

'And the excuses customers give when they're caught. Half of 'em say they've read 3 OFF as 30 FF. Did you ever! Others pretend they've read the price upside-down and merely stuck their own label on to make the figuring more legible for the cashiers. So we've got a strict rule in this store never to mark anything at 61, 81, 86, 91, 98, 99p and so on. That 99p is incredible: we have at least a dozen rogues every week who insist that it's 66.'

'How frightful!' I said. 'I'd no idea customers could get up to such tricks.'

'Some of the things I could tell you, squire,' he said, 'you wouldn't believe. We had one customer who got away with murder for nearly six moths. She had her own labels, but she avoided suspicion by telling the cashiers that her weekly tin of corned beef had come from our "This Week's Bargain" stand where we offer goods looking slightly the worse for wear. Then one day our store detective caught her red-handed – and red-faced with the effort – making a big dent in a tin of corned beef with an outsize pair of pliers. There she was, behind the cereals display, straining to make her purchase look like damaged goods. Clever? I'll say she was clever. She was an artist in her way. Every tin looked a natural "transit casualty" when she'd finished with it.'

'Amazing!' I said. 'Well, thank you, Mr Pendlebury, for being so courteous and giving me so much of your time.'

He took me by the elbow and propelled me to the dairy produce aisle.

'Have a go at this,' he said, handing me a Dutch cheese marked at 58p. 'It's a new idea we're trying. An assistant window dresser put it in our Suggestion Box last week.'

I studied the cheese and the label and could see nothing odd.

'Remove the top label,' he said.

I did so and read the message underneath. 'You're being watched!' it said. And just above the lettering there was a tiny drawing of a set of hand-cuffs.